IT HAD TO HAPPEN

MEMOIRS FROM A FOSTER CHILD:
ABANDONED

Mattie L. Williams

DEDICATION

To the brave and resilient souls who have journeyed through the shadows of foster care, facing the harrowing challenges of abuse and trauma. This book is a testament to the strength within each of you—survivors who have carried the weight of untold stories and endured the pain in silence. You are not alone.

This dedication extends to the young foster hearts unfairly judged, labeled, or misunderstood. Your worth is not defined by the circumstances that brought you here, but by the resilience that propels you forward. May this book stand as a beacon of hope, reminding you that your past does not dictate your future.

Remember, you possess the power to overcome, to heal, and to rise above the shadows. You are not defined by the scars of the past; rather, they are testaments to your strength. As you navigate the pages of this book, may you find solace, understanding, and the unwavering belief that you can not only survive but thrive. Your journey is unique, but in these words, may you discover the shared strength that binds us together.

To the possibility of healing, growth, and success—may this book be a companion on your path. You are not alone. Live in the present for your future!

TABLE OF CONTENTS

FOREWORD

Peace is defined as freedom from disturbance and a sense of tranquility, but so many young people and even older people lack peace because they cannot release the past or are living in fear of the future. Galatians 5:22 says, "Peace is the fruit of the Holy Spirit." Giving voice to the things you carry is where peace starts. Mattie, your voice has grown stronger over the years, and your words have provided a space for others to know they do not walk alone. "It Had to Happen, Memoirs from A Foster Child" Book 2, opening closed doors and reliving memories, is the quiet after the storm.

Mattie L. Williams shares her experience not to cast clouds but to let the readers know that you have peace of mind waiting for you, and the first step is to release. The power of your words can change the course of so many lives, but couple that with the power of God's words, and watch your life take off to new heights with peace leading the way.

One final thought, family comes in many different packages. Find the right package for you and dig in! Mattie, thank you for sharing your life and love with me.

I am so proud of you!

Aunt Steph

INTRODUCTION

In the delicate dance between shadows and resilience, the pages of "It Had To Happen: Memoirs From A Foster Child: Abandoned" reveal the profound odyssey of Tameena. This is not merely a memoir but an invitation to traverse the labyrinth of survival, strength, and the unyielding spirit that refuses to be silenced. Step into Tameena's world, where the echoes of an abusive family propel her into the unforgiving embrace of the foster care system. Shattered sanctuary and fractured familial bonds become the backdrop for a journey that transcends pain and emerges as a testament to the power of resilience.

Tameena's story begins with the promise of safety in a foster home, only to be met with a betrayal that threatens to unravel her newfound sense of security. As she navigates the complex tapestry of her own resilience, secrets become her silent companions, and faith becomes both shield and refuge. This memoir is a poignant exploration of survival etched in the pages of Tameena's journals—each entry a silent scream for release from the weight of unspeakable pain. Through the harrowing cycles of abuse within the foster care system, Tameena's spirit remains unbroken, and her determination to seek justice becomes a guiding light.

"It Had To Happen" is a raw narrative, an unfiltered lens into the failings of a system meant to protect vulnerable children. Tameena's resilience is not just her own; it is a call to action, demanding that we confront systemic issues and champion the healing and empowerment of survivors. As you embark on this journey, prepare to witness the emergence of strength from the darkest corners of adversity. Tameena's story is a rallying cry for change, a collective stand against the definition that trauma seeks to impose. This is not just her journey; it's an exploration that beckons us all to say, "It had to happen, but it will not define me."

CHAPTER ONE
STRANGERS IN A NEW HOME

"Alright girls, we're here!" Ms. Casey said in a cheery but dragging way as the big white DHS van came to a stop in front of a red and white house. Lyfe, Fifi, Sophie, and I were the last to be dropped off after stopping at two other homes to drop off my nieces and nephew. *Man, that was very hard for everyone to accept.* When we dropped off my niece and nephew Lei'Lynn and Damir at their foster home, they were crying and holding on to me, not letting me go. The good thing for Lei'Lynn and Damir is that they are siblings with the same mother but different daddies, and luckily able to stay together and live in the same foster home. Even though they would be together, I knew their pain because they were already taken away from their mother; my sister Regina (Gina) when they were two and three years old. Like my mother, Gina was abusive to Lei'Lynn and Damir. One day Gina beat Damir because he peed on himself. She beat Damir so badly that she broke his arms and legs. I remember it like it was yesterday because as a child myself who was probably six or seven years old, I thought Damir's arms and legs were off his body, *y'all judging me I know lol. I had dreams of him being chopped up into pieces for years before I understood the concept of broken bones in the body.* Lei'Lynn and Damir had already been through a lot and now they are being taken away from their grandmother, my mother, and given into the hands of complete, and hopefully good strangers. Thinking about this was all too much to handle at one time. To get my niece and nephew to exit the van, Ms. Casey had to pry their little hands and arms from around my sisters and me to release their grips.

I was heartbroken, my sisters were heartbroken, and even the adults in the van seemed to have had a hard time with what they were witnessing, but they were trained to keep it together as part of the job. When they exited the van, I just bawled my eyes out as the pain was too much to hold on to; I wasn't as strong as I thought I was at that moment, and this was just the first stop. I tried to leap out of the van, but one of the ladies in the van stopped me saying, "Tameena you cannot leave the van!" as she pulled me closer to her while Ms. Casey closed the sliding door to the van. As soon as the door closed, I heard the hard "chuck" sound of the driver locking the van door. The sound was louder than usual. It was as if I were the only one in the van, trapped with a blindfold on, tied up, and unable to use any other sense but hearing. The sound was so final and absolute that I couldn't hold back my tears. During the time Ms. Casey took Lei'Lynn and Damir into their new home — which seemed like hours but took about 10 minutes — Lyfe and Fifi had some words in the van.

"That's fucked up, we can't even get out of the van to say goodbye!" Lyfe blurted out.

Fifi, being Fifi, echoed Lyfe's outburst with a twist. "Right like, that's fucked up, we can't even get out of the van, what type of shit is that?" Ignoring their rants, I just sat crying bent over with my face in my hands as Lei'Lynn and Damir struggled into their new home.

Ms. Casey returned to the van with no speech or anything, maybe she thought of just rip the band-aid right off, because we just pulled off, and drove on to the next home to drop my niece Rachel off at her foster home; she was going to be by herself. Rachel was the only child of my sister Lisa. Well, not quite the only child, but the only child as far as Rachel knew. Lisa had another child named Thomas before Rachel was born. Lisa put Thomas up for adoption when he was born and hadn't told Rachel, so she had never met him or heard of him before. So, she had no other family member go with her to her new home, and that made me even more sad and angry at the same time.

"How is she just going to be alone like that? She can't just come with us?" I cried aloud, talking to no specific person, but hoping Ms. Casey would reconsider.

Ms. Casey just responded, "I'm sorry Tameena, this is how it must be for now. Rachel will be well taken care of by her new guardians."

On the ride to drop Rachel off, I held onto her tightly with my right arm around the back of her neck and my left hand holding her left hand, weeping silently, hoping that she knew what the knot in my throat wouldn't allow me to say. I was saying *that I loved her, that it would be okay, and that we would be reunited again.* When we arrived in front of Rachel's foster home, it was like déjà vu from the last drop-off. Rachel did not want to let me go, and neither did I, but again we had to be released from each other's grip. My heart broke again. I never understood how my heart could break so much in one day. Although I knew what was happening, I knew what was coming, but I wasn't ready to experience that same pain again so soon. Rachel cried her way into the stranger's home while holding Ms. Casey's hand and looking back, hopelessly, at the van with its tinted windows. I hoped she knew that although she couldn't see me, I could see her and that I watched as she went all the way into the house as if it were the last act of protection from me.

It was silent the whole van ride from dropping off Rachel, as Lyfe, Fifi, Sophie, and I were driven to our new home — the red and white stranger's house. By that time, I think I was all cried out, like I literally didn't have any more tears for the day. I'm sure my face showed the pain I felt. It felt like maybe God had allotted me a specific amount of tears for this specific day, and I had used them all on my nieces and nephew. I didn't have enough for me; after all, I could handle myself. I was used to caring for myself anyway. When I cried a lot, my face would look pale, and my eyes would get red for a while after I finished crying. As we rolled down this unleveled street with train tracks, we finally arrived at our destination in Southwest Philly. The block was "hot"; there were people sitting outside on their porches, adults, and children. The children were playing and running up and down the street. It reminded me of my block in North Philly, except this time around I hoped I would be able to participate. I was glad that I was going to be in a better home where I wasn't getting the daylight beaten out of me, but the shock of being away from my mother made it difficult for me to adapt.

As we got out of the van to approach the red and white house, there were three men standing in front of the house talking. When we reached the front of the stairs, one of the men yelled, "Momma I think they're here!" Before we could go up the stairs, we were greeted by an elderly woman who had just walked out of the house. This woman was short, brown-skinned, wore glasses, and had long salt and pepper hair, but there was more pepper than salt that fell to her shoulders. "Oh hi, c-c-c-come on in, and please e-e-e-excuse my sons, the-they're here visiting me," the elderly woman stuttered.

This had been the first time I'd heard someone stutter. I thought she was just talking fast because she was excited but later learned that she had a speech impediment. Ms. Casey followed behind the elderly woman, and my sisters and I followed behind Ms. Casey. entering the house, there was a square-shaped vestibule with another door to walk through before getting inside the actual house. Once inside the house, the first thing I noticed was the red carpet on the floor, which reminded me of the red carpet at my mother's house. I was already uneasy and ashamed that I had to live with a complete stranger because my mother didn't love me, but now I was afraid of the red carpet. *I hated red carpets because they reminded me of physical pain and its ability to disguise blood.* I was filled with so many raging emotions of anxiety, anger, and fear, but I concealed those emotions in my head. I couldn't break down now; I had to be strong for Sophie who cried throughout the entire meet and greet. The red carpet traveled from the living room to the dining room, stopping at the threshold of the kitchen in the back. The setup of the house seemed to be exactly like the setup of my mother's house which felt like torture.

"Please have a s-seat," the elderly woman suggested, as she pointed to the chairs at the dining room table.

"Thank you so much again Ms. Martry for caring for these children! This is Lyfe, Tameena, Phoenix, and Sephora," Ms. Casey introduced.

We all responded in unison, "Hi."

"And I-I-I am Ms. Martry, but you can call me Gr-Grandmo," Ms. Martry added as she gave us all a hug.

At the sight of her moving close to us, Fifi and I flinched a little because we were the last ones to know what a hug felt like. My mother didn't give out hugs; instead, she gave out punches and one-way flights down the stairs, especially to me and Fifi.

After the meet and greet, Ms. Casey asked Ms. Martry if she could show us our rooms and where we would be sleeping. Ms. Martry took us upstairs and to my surprise, the upstairs of the house was just the same layout as the upstairs of my mother's house. The stairs were in front of the door. There was a front room where Ms. Martry slept, which was the same outline as my mother's room. Then there were three more rooms with the same layout as our old rooms. There was a small room next to Ms. Martry's room which was set up with a bed and some dark tote bins. That room was supposed to be "the room no one slept in." *Turned out that one of her sons was living there but wasn't supposed to because he wasn't cleared to live with children by DHS; he was on drugs.* Next to that room was a bathroom, and then two rooms on the right of the bathroom. Ms. Martry walked us to each room and stopped at the room next to the bathroom, which was going to be Fifi and Sophie's. Their room was spacious with a set of bunked beds to the left and a wide dresser to the right. The room had a connecting door to the back room just like the rooms at my mother's house, but the bunked beds here were blocking the entrance of that door. We walked to the back room where Lyfe and I would sleep, it had a set of bunked beds with the bottom bunk bigger than the top bunk. The window in the middle of the room gave me flashbacks of my mother's house with Fifi's head going out of the window. I thought to myself, *how am I going to survive it here, if everything looked the same at home?* After that thought, I started a new facade that nothing bothered me. It was the only way I was going to live here peacefully.

19

Shortly after the walk-through of the home Ms. Casey left, but before she left, she grouped us altogether to tell us that this living arrangement was only temporary.

"Listen, I know this doesn't feel good right now, but you will be able to visit your mother soon enough. You may even be able to go back to live with her again. She just has to get help first, and I am going to help her with what she needs," Ms. Casey explained.

I noticed as she was explaining all this, Sophie's eyes lit up like she couldn't wait to see and live with my mother again. I, on the other hand, knew it was too early to have such great hopes. *Sure, Mother was just gonna suddenly learn how to not beat my ass for no apparent reason,* I thought sarcastically. I couldn't see the metamorphosis just yet. Although I wanted my mother to change, hearing about it was all too soon to believe that it could happen.

Fifi blurted out what I was thinking, "I ain't going back there so she can beat the shit out of me again! Look what she did to me!" pointing to the scars on her head.

As you can see, this pep talk wasn't going so well, but the gist of it is that we would have visitations with my mother when she

20

was able. It was an emotional rollercoaster. One minute I was crying, filled with shame, and sadness because I was being torn apart from my family, and the next minute I was relieved and angry at the thought of reunification. Ms. Casey encouraged us to be strong and behave while we were at our new home before she left. That seemed like a stretch for Lyfe, but for some reason, I had faith in her and thought that she would be better while we were here, because there wasn't anyone cussing us out, or beating the crap out of us. Unfortunately, I was sadly mistaken. Lyfe and Fifi really showed their behinds while Sophie and I did our best to follow the rules.

CHAPTER TWO
CHANGES

There was a lot of change happening so fast and all at once that my sisters and I had to get used to it when we moved into Ms. Martyr's house. We had to get used to living with a stranger, attending new schools, making new friends, and learning how to be children in our new neighborhood. Ms. Martry was lovely. She bought us NEW clothes, fed us every day at least twice a day and a few snacks in between, and didn't beat the crap out of us. So, in my mind because she treated me better than my mother, she was family. Sophie and I started to call her grandma after a few weeks of living there, but Lyfe and Fifi continued to call her Ms. Martry. We were all still trying to get used to living with a stranger in her house and living by her rules, so giving the stranger a personable name made it seem more like home to me. To Lyfe and Fifi, using personable names seemed like disrespect to our mother. When they called her Ms. Martry, she would say, "You know you can call me Grandma" and they would respond "You ain't my Grandma!" with an attitude attached. Even sometimes when I would call her grandma, Lyfe would get mad at me saying, "You know damn well that ain't yo' Grandma, you don't even know her like that!" Although this was true, and Grandma let everyone know we were her foster children, *which made me feel a little ashamed*, she took good care of us and made us feel like we were part of her family. *At least calling her grandma made me feel like family anyway.*

Besides, it was the hard truth that we were her foster children, and no matter what we called her, she wasn't our family. Although we weren't blood, Ms. Martry and her family accepted us and treated us like kin, and it felt kind of good to be a part of a "functional" family, *whatever that means*. It was something I never had, but something I wanted to be a part of badly. So, despite Lyfe and Fifi's reluctance, I continued to call Ms. Martry Grandma.

Living with Grandma, everything was different from the way I used to live when I was with my mother. The atmosphere was more peaceful inside the house, and outside of the house was a little calmer too, *just a little because we were still in a hood, it was just a different hood*. Inside the house, there wasn't so much yelling and hands-on approaches to discipline at all. At Grandma's house, we could talk, listen to music, watch TV, and be children. When we weren't listening, Grandma would simply tell us to stop, and quiet down, and sometimes, she would raise her voice, but it was not even close to things we used to hear back home. At my mom's home, we couldn't talk or listen to music, unless it was with her when she was a good drunk, and we weren't able to watch TV much. Somehow when we did, my mother would yell, "Shut up all that damn noise" or she would call us names like "you dirty, stanky hussie" and sometimes she would call us "bitches." To this day, I hate the word "bitch" as a term of endearment among friends, mainly girls who are friends. The word was used so much to degrade me; I can't imagine why friends call each other that for fun. Grandma never called us names, even if we were misbehaving and such, she calmly explained what we were doing wrong and reinforced us to do the right thing. We were able to go outside and play with the kids on the block. *There were a lot of kids on the block.* It wasn't just the 4th of July either that we were able to play outside, because *that was the only time my mother would let us play outside.* At Grandma's, we played outside almost every day when the weather was good. To be honest, I was having a hard time acclimating to this safe and secure freedom.

The first year my sisters and I were there, we didn't have household chores, *well we did have to keep our rooms clean,* but other than that, we didn't have any major chores around the house as we did at my mother's house. At my mother's house, Fifi and I did most of the cleaning, but I was Cinderella in real-time flesh. I dusted, swept, mopped, washed dishes, did laundry, and wiped down walls and woodwork. I don't know if Grandmom thought we didn't know how to clean or not, but she didn't ask us to and that was great because I needed the break, or *maybe the social worker told her how much we used to clean and asked her to give us a break with cleaning for a while?* Anyway, Grandma would get up on Saturdays and clean her house, and I would sit around and watch as she missed spots and didn't clean the woodwork! *It took everything in me not to tell her she missed a spot, and don't forget about the woodwork.* Instead, I just marveled at the fact that it wasn't me doing all the cleaning this time. *Oh, what a dutiless year it had been!*

Cinderella, out!! Besides, there were other and more important things to focus on besides chores, like feeling safe and trying to embrace safety.

It took me some time to adjust to being away from my mother and feeling a sense of safety. The first few times I was able to play outside, I was stiff. I felt like I was in prison for so long that on my first day out, I just took in the air and sunlight as I looked over my shoulder to make sure my mother wasn't going to show up. Although I was in a safer environment, I was constantly worried that my mother was lurking around me. It's like I was waiting for the sound of my mother's car to turn down the block so I could run into the house as if I had snuck outside or something. It didn't matter where I was; I could be at home, outside, or at school, I just didn't feel like I was completely safe from my mother. It didn't matter about the people who were around me — Grandma, social workers, teachers, or friends — I didn't feel protected, because I was still anxious about being captured by my mother. There were times when I went outside and was afraid that she was going to show up and steal me away from Grandma. As I spent more time outside and realized my mother wasn't coming for me, the sense of unease gradually subsided. I started to feel like we didn't have to sneak out to go to the playground. All summer long, my grandma would let us walk around the block to go to the playground by ourselves and tell us to be back before the streetlights came on. When summer ended and school started, everything changed.

It was time for my sisters and I to start our new schools. Sophie did not have to change schools, as she was able to continue attending Widener Memorial School for students with disabilities and was bused from Grandma's house to school. Lyfe attended West Philadelphia High School — *well, she was registered to attend but didn't show up*, and Fifi and I attended Shaw Middle School, *and she was also registered to attend but didn't go*. Some things didn't change with Lyfe as she continued to skip school. She dropped out of high school because she just stopped going. Following her big sister's footsteps, Fifi skipped school and dropped out of middle school. I continued to attend school because I didn't want to be like my mother or my sisters, who were closely becoming my mother. If I wanted anything better in life, I knew I had to work hard for it, starting with attending school. School was always an outlet for me anyway, especially when I was living with my mother. Now school was fun for me. It was a time I could meet new friends, be sociable, and be a child for once without the worries of getting in trouble every day, yet the fear of my mother lingered throughout the rest of my life.

I didn't get into too much trouble at school, but when I did get into trouble, I thought the school was going to call my mother instead of calling my grandma. The first time I got in trouble at school was after a few months at Shaw, and it was for passing a note back and forth with this boy named Marcus. I was sitting at my desk when, I saw Marcus's arm reach over to me with a folded-up piece of paper in his hand. At first, I just looked at him with a blank stare like, *what do you want? I don't know you.* Marcus started pushing his hand back and forth, but low under the table like he was sneaking and as to say *Take it, take it.* Then I snatched the paper out of his hand, opened it on the top of my desk *because I didn't realize we were sneaking around,* and read it quietly to myself. I had never passed notes in class before, and no one ever really liked me that much to do that in my other middle schools. On top of that, I was absent a lot due to getting suspended for half of the school year. The paper read, "Do you like me, yes or no?" with a box under the words *yes* and *no*. I looked over at him, looked him up and down to check him out, then got my pencil and made another box next to no and wrote "maybe" above it. I figured I'd entertain the foolery. Marcus was light-skinned with hazel brown eyes, and a box haircut. Light skin was in, so I checked the *maybe* box and passed the paper back to him for him to grab. The class was full of about twenty-four students with my desk seat to the left of his, and we sat in the middle of the classroom. After Marcus took the note back, he wrote something on it and passed it back to me. The note read, "I want to kiss you. Do you want to kiss me?" with a *yes* and *no* box for me to check. I looked at him like he had two heads and wrote "ewww" with a box under it that I checked. Before I could fully pass the note back to him, my teacher Ms. M. walked over to my desk and took the note out of my hand, unfolded it, read it quietly, and said to me, "You come with me!" For some reason I was the only one who had to go with the teacher. I guess because I was the last one with the note. A message to educators: *there are always two sides to a story, a situation, and an incident, so please listen to both sides of the story before reprimanding a student. Not only is it not fair, but it makes that student feel useless and it creates a ripple effect of unwanted useless behaviors in that student. Sometimes, it's not what you say or do to the student, it's how you make the student feel that encourages all behavioral outcomes, positive or negative.*

Ms. M and I walked out of the classroom, and she scolded me saying, "You need to stop being fresh. You should not be passing nasty notes in class!"

"But he passed the note to me first. I was just answering the note!" I said timidly but annoyed.

"Tameena, you mean to tell me he wrote this note to you, and not the other way around?" she asked with the notion that I was not telling the truth.

"Yes Ms. M.," I responded while sucking my teeth and rolling my eyes.

"I am going to have to call your mom and let her know of your inappropriate behavior!" Ms. M scolded.

As soon as Ms. M. mentioned my mother I started to freak out. "Please don't call my mom, I don't live with her anymore, I am not allowed to see her anymore. I am so sorry Ms. M. It won't happen again, I promise!" I exclaimed with tears in my eyes.

"Tameena, calm down! Who is your guardian? I will call them!" Ms. M said, puzzled.

Wiping the tears from my eyes, I responded, "I live with my grandma", as I gave her the house number.

I had my first panic attack in front of my teacher, but I was so relieved to know that she wasn't going to call my mother. Thank God we were in the hallway and not in the classroom, where my classmates would see me freaking out. A message to my fellow educators: *Do your research on the students you teach. At least find out the basics of the student, like who they live with, their age, and something they like and dislike. There are so many students, like me, who have experienced parental trauma, and as a result, do not live with their biological parents. Every student doesn't live with a mother and a father, some students live with a grandparent or an aunt, some students are homeless, or they live with a foster parent.*

It is imperative to know who the guardians are of each of your students to prevent potential post-traumatic stress anxiety attacks, like the many I had growing up in foster care. Although I was relieved that Ms. M was not calling my mother and was calling my grandma instead, I was still anxious. This was my first time getting a call home and even though Grandma never put her hands on me, out of habit I expected to be cussed out or brutally beaten. I thought adults had to beat children when they misbehaved. Grandma was different; she never put her hands on me; however, she did tell me how disappointed in me she was, but she never raised her hand to me, ever. It was a relief to know I had the freedom to make mistakes without strenuous repercussions and that I had the ability to live like a normal child, at least now.

CHAPTER THREE
VISITATIONS

I had not seen my mother for about six months because she was in jail for the incident of beating Fifi so badly to the point of hospitalization. When she got out of jail my sisters and I were able to have supervised visits at the foster care agency. Grandma would get us all up early like around 7 a.m. on a Saturday — *which wasn't ideal for a twelve-year-old, I loved to sleep* — and we got dressed to go visit my mother twice a month. Traveling there was a lot, we had to catch a trolley, the El train, and a bus to get to the program, just to sit in my mother's empty presence. I remember waiting anxiously and fearfully for my mother to show up at the program. I hated going to the program because the décor of the building depicted images and words that seemed elusive to me. I would be waiting in a colorful and decorated room with posters of families sitting at a table laughing and playing games. Anchor charts full of family quotes that looked and sounded cheesy as if every family was meant to be healthy and functional. The room was separated by activities, toys, and games to play as a family. It looked like a big classroom that could fit about ten families at once. The waiting room was filled with foster children waiting for their biological parents to enter. As some parents walked into the room to meet with their children, I watched their children's eyes light up at the sight of their parents' entrance. Some of the children would run over to their parents and give them a big hug, some parents cried at the sight of seeing their children when entering the room, and some children just waited patiently for their parents to join the room. When my mother walked into the room for our visits, Sophie seemed to be the only one who was excited, her eyes the only ones lit at the sight of our mother. At first, Lyfe didn't show much. I don't think she could face my mother with all that carrying-on she was doing at Grandma's house. Eventually, Lyfe loosened up and was able to have light conversations with our mother. Fifi and I were still afraid of our mother; our eyes looked at each other most of the time or down at the floor when we saw her. It was like the struggle connected us because we shared so many beatings and punishments together. No matter how uncomfortable my visits were with my mother, the visits continued for about a year.

Visiting started to get a little easier for me, although I still didn't fancy having to get up early two Saturdays each month. When we first started our visits, it was a little awkward. I didn't know what to say, how to feel, or even how to act around my mother. Fear of our past history stopped me from seeing that my mother was trying to get herself together, so she could get us back. She didn't necessarily make it easy for me either because sometimes I saw anger in her eyes. All I could remember was, "If I ever go to jail for you, I will kill you myself!" My mother used to say this to Fifi and me, and it stuck with me. She definitely went to jail for a few months after we were taken away, so I thought that was her plan for me. I thought she was *going to act as if she wanted me back so she could get me and start where she left off, which was beating the crap out of me and turning me back into the role of the cleaning Cinderella. Maybe she will take me back and this time, lock me in a room with no food or water until I die.* Those were the thoughts in my mind for the first few visits. As our visits continued, we would talk, but the conversations would be short, just basic greetings like, "Hi, how are you? How is school? Are you being good?" These were the type of questions my mother would ask. In return, I would answer "Hi Mommy, I am good. School is good. Yes, ma'am I am being good." still with fear in my heart. It got easier to answer her questions as each visit passed. As we continued to visit, my mother was getting closer and closer to winning us back. She had to take a parenting class and make all or most of her visits. Although she did everything right on paper to get us back, I was still very much afraid of her and had very little faith that her behavior would utterly change; that miraculously she was healed from alcoholism and beating the shit out of me. I just didn't have that much faith in her or the system yet, and I was new to the Christian faith and did not believe in miracles.

Visiting our mother wasn't the only visitation we had; we also had visitations with our social worker. She visited us once a month, at least she was supposed to visit us once a month as "Well-being" checks, but she only visited once every three months, it seemed. Our social worker would only come to visit when there was a problem between Grandma, Lyfe, and Fifi. She would come and tell Lyfe and Fifi to behave or they would have to be taken and placed into a different foster home, but they continued to keep up with their shenanigans. After about 11 months of being in foster care, on this one visit, our social worker showed up because she had "great news" for us.

"Your mother has completed every step to get you back home and is ready to take you back as soon as next week!" our social worker said excitedly.

We were all sitting at the dining room table when she told us this news. Thank God I was already sitting because I broke down into a mini panic attack in my head.

Meanwhile, Sophie was so elated she started smiling from ear to ear, saying, "Yes, we're going home" while balling up both fists and raising her arms in the air from left to right simultaneously.

"I am not going back there!" Lyfe blurted, breaking Sophie's celebration.

"I'm not either!" Fifi added.

"I don't want to go back!" I continued as I buried my head down to my chest.

"What do you mean? That's our mother! I want to go back home!" Sophie cried.

The social worker intervened with, "Well, technically, you don't have to go back as long as you are allowed to stay here, or you will be placed in another home. You have time to think about it, from now until next week and then I'll be back."

It was the saddest but most relieving thing at the same time, to know that I had a choice whether to stay in foster care or go and live with my mother. Honestly, it was one of the hardest decisions I had to make in my life, but at the time it seemed right to just stay put. To leave would be like leaving a burning building and running back in to save my security blanket or something. I didn't want to put myself back into the line of fire. Sophie didn't have too much to be afraid of because she got off easy regarding punishments and beatings by dint of her disability. On the other hand, I have felt the sting of my mother's wrath and I was not fittna, *yeah, I said fittna,* feel that again, for potentially the rest of my life. Sorrowfully, I understood where Sophie came from as well, but couldn't concur with her decision to leave and move back in with our mother. My mind was made up, and to me the decision was more detrimental to my health than to Sophie's.

Next week came and so did Ms. Casey with her plastic bags again. She came with enough bags for each of us to have our own. I helped Sophie pack her bag as I asked her repeatedly, "Are you sure you want to go back to live with Mommy?"

Sophie responded, "Yes, I am sure I want to live with Mommy! Are you sure you don't want to go back home too?"

After some quick thoughts about how life used to be with my mother, the bad thoughts outweighed the good ones, so I responded, "Yes, I'm sure. I don't want to get beat on anymore," as I shook my head trying to get those images of me getting beaten out of my mind.

"I will miss you, Sis, but I know we will be visiting you guys at the program," Sophie said.

"I will miss you too, Sis," I responded.

As we continued to get Sophie together, I got really emotional about her leaving. I didn't show it because I didn't want her to be sad, so I held in my emotions. Fifi folded up Sophie's wheelchair, and I picked Sophie up and took her out to the white DHS Van. As I was carrying her, I felt scared for Sophie, I really didn't want her to go back to my mother because I didn't want my mother to hurt her as she hurt me. There were so many different reasons that flashed before my eyes as to why I didn't want Sophie to go. The most important one being, I thought my mother would be so mad at me for not moving back in with her that she would take it out on Sophie and start treating her the way she treated me. That thought terrified me so much that I contemplated running inside the house to pack a bag, so I could go back just to take care of Sophie, but I just couldn't. It was just a contemplation; I didn't act on it but I was close. Instead, I just let Sophie go. This was the first time I had to let go of someone so I could live a better life. This decision was so hard for me because I didn't just let Sophie go, I was also letting my mother go as well. I was used to bearing the brunt of everything, protecting others to save them, hoping for better to come while I was out struggling to survive. This time, I chose myself, and although at that moment I felt terrible, looking back on my decision, I believed it was one of the best choices I've ever had to make.

Although I wasn't ready to face my mother for not going back to live with her, I wanted to see Sophie; I needed to know that she was OK, so I attended the visitations. Sophie and my mother came to visit a few times at the program, but after a while, they stopped showing up to visit with Lyfe, Fifi, and me. The last visit was awkwardly intense because my mother just sat there, not saying hi or anything like she just came to drop Sophie off. She slouched in the chair with her elbows on her knees and her hand on her chin. Her lips were tight and her face frowned a little. It was scary. I thought she was just going to open up a can of butt-whooping right there in the program. Sophie on the other hand was elated to see us as her eyes lit up at the sight of us, and our eyes to her presence. As we started talking to Sophie, who could talk a mile a minute. I couldn't help but keep stealing a glance at my mother, wondering *what she was thinking about, how come she is not talking, is she not happy to see us?* I wanted to speak to her but I was afraid and didn't want to push my luck, so I just continued to talk to Sophie until our visit was over. When our visit ended, Lyfe, Fifi, Sophie, and I said our goodbyes, and see you next time, *not knowing that this was going to be the last time we saw them for* years. Meanwhile, my mother just stood behind Sophie silently with her hands resting on the handles of Sophie's wheelchair, ready to wheel her away. At our last farewell, my mother turned Sophie around and wheeled her away, still not saying a word. Sophie with her back turned to us waved goodbye over her wheelchair, and the rest of us waved back to Sophie. It was all so weird that I thought about that day for the next few days, trying to figure out what was happening with my mother, but couldn't put my finger on it. Maybe my mother wasn't good at goodbyes.

On the next scheduled visit, Lyfe, Fifi, and I showed up at the program waiting for my mother to enter the room, and after about 20 minutes of waiting one of the social workers came in and told us that my mother hadn't called to let them know if she was coming or not and that my sisters and I had the choice to leave with Grandma and go back home. Lyfe and Fifi always voted to leave right away. I wanted to stay just in case I could get to see Sophie, but the majority ruled and we left the program. Lyfe and Fifi didn't want to see my mother because they had so much unwarranted freedom that they didn't earn or deserve. I didn't want to see my mother because I was still very much afraid of her and wasn't ready to face her again after the Great Separation. Even though I didn't want to see my mother, she could still have put in the effort to visit us. *Maybe she just didn't care about us that much anyway and was glad we didn't come back. What if she hates me? Maybe she never loved me,* I thought as I sat waiting for her to show up. There were so many negative thoughts that ran through my mind, and because of those thoughts, I begged Grandma to stay home, and never go to an empty visit again, and she agreed. After the first few times, my mother bailed out on me, I chose to do the same, and I never went to another visit.

After the last visit, I hadn't spoken to or seen my mother or any of my sisters for about ten years, and I was missing my family badly. I had been experiencing hard times in my foster homes and was praying for my family to get back together. Ten years after the last visit, I decided I was going to just show up at the house and see if my mother and Sophie were home. During the ten-year gap, I met a wonderful lady from church who I still call to this day my Aunt

Sandrine (Aunt Sandi). Aunt Sandi was there for me through a lot of my traumatic experiences and helped me in the healing process, encouraging me to do better for myself. As part of my healing process, I wanted to see my mother and all my sisters, but I only knew where my mother and Sophie lived. Lyfe and Fifi were off the radar; I didn't know where they were. I didn't know whether they were in a home, or on the run, so I knew I wasn't going to be able to visit them at this time. I just wanted to see my mother and Sophie and start the reunification of my family. Aunt Sandi thought it was a good idea and she drove me to my mother's house and stayed with me during the visit.

When I reached my mother's house and knocked on the door, all I could do was pray that someone would answer the door. My mother answered the door saying, "Who is it?" in her friendly but not-so-friendly voice.

"It's Meena Mommy," I replied in an excited but nervous voice.

My mother opened the door in her housecoat and her hair stuck up all over the place. It didn't matter to me because I was just so happy to see her and know that she was alive.

"Come on in," she said as she let Aunt Sandi and me in the house. There was no big hug, no *I missed you*, no big hurrah. It was just "Come on in." As soon as I walked through the door, I saw Sophie sitting across the room in her wheelchair, and I ran over to her and gave her a big hug and kiss.

"Oh, my God, you're here," Sophie said with a big smile on her face.

"I know, I missed you guys so much I had to come and visit," I responded.

I then walked over to my mother and gave her a hug, and she hugged me back.

I introduced my Aunt Sandi to my mother and Sophie, "Mommy and Sophie, this is my Aunt Sandi."

My Aunt Sandi responded, "It is so nice to finally meet you. Meena has been talking about you guys for a while, and I wanted her to see you guys!" When I looked over at my mother, I could tell she was uneasy about me introducing Aunt Sandi as Aunt Sandi because her face frowned for a second and then went back to a fake smirk.

The visit was short and sweet because the house was a mess. The house smelt like a porta potty, and it was filled with dirty dishes, clothes, and other things my mother hoarded in the living room and dining room. It caught me by surprise because when I was living with my mother, she made sure we cleaned the house every day. *Now that I think about it, maybe the house was a mess because I wasn't there to clean it, huh?* Aunt Sandi was clean and neat, she didn't eat or sit at people's houses when they were a mess. She kind of just stood in the middle of the room, but she was not going to leave me alone in there with my mother. Surprisingly, we didn't have much to talk about. I didn't feel comfortable telling my mother all the bad things that happened to me in foster care because of her negligence, but I did get a chance to talk with her and Sophie for a little bit about school and stuff. Then I was ready to go because it just became awkward; I was running out of positive stories to tell.

"Well Mommy, it was nice seeing you. Sophie, it was nice seeing you, and I love you both."

"I love you, too!" Both my mother and Sophie responded.

I walked out of the door, not seeing my mother or Sophie again for about another seven years.

Time passed by, and I had only seen my mother and Sophie a few times in 17 years. I remember two times when my Aunt Sandi picked Sophie up and took us out to eat. There was this other time when one of my cousins from my foster family picked Sophie up so she could go to Clementon Park with our church. That was fun, but it all ended there; I didn't see her again until I was well into my 30s. Looking back on this time and after talking with Sophie, I think my mother was hurt that I chose not to go back to live with her, and that could have been the reason why she didn't show up to our visits and never called. I always wondered if I had done the right thing by not going back with my mother, but her absence confirmed that I had made the right choice.

CHAPTER FOUR
MEETING MY BESTIE!

It was my first day of 6th grade at Shaw Middle School when I met a girl named Yanisha Jordan. Yanisha was light-skinned with long dark hair which flowed past her shoulders, falling to the middle of her back. We were in the same class and sat at the same group of desks. The desks were the old square wooden desks with chairs that didn't attach. They were set up in blocks of four desks per group. Yanisha was sitting across from me diagonally, and one sitting next to us on our left. Yanisha looked like she was excited to be at school and introduced herself to me.

"Hi, I'm Yanisha, but you can call me Yani," she said as she waved hi to me.

"Hey, I'm Tameena, but you can call me Meena" I replied excitedly but hesitant to meet Yani, waving back.

The weirdest thing happened: We just started laughing for no reason. We were both so silly and excited to start school and meet a new friend, I guess it made us laugh. We laughed at people, at ourselves, and at whatever was going on around us; we were so silly. Surprisingly Yani and I had totally different personalities, but somehow, she made me feel comfortable enough to laugh and live in the moment — something I didn't usually do before meeting Yani.

Yani and I were both new to Shaw Middle School, but she knew some of the other kids at Shaw. She knew kids from the neighborhood elementary school she attended and knew kids who lived on her block who attended Shaw as well. I was new to the school and the neighborhood, so I didn't know anyone except Yani. It wasn't as easy for me to make friends as it was for Yani because she had a bubbly personality, where she gave everyone the benefit of the doubt and was super friendly. I was a little outgoing but reserved at the same time. My personality was based on the feeling I got when I met someone. If you looked at me wrong it was going to be a problem. If I felt like you were going to be a problem for me in any way, I didn't bang (like, hang around) with you, and at some point, might be a problem. Some of the people Yani was friends with I didn't even like, but since I hung around Yani, I hung around them and was cordial. I was good at making friends, but I just didn't trust everyone. I had to flex a little bit on some of the students so they knew not to play with me. There were times when I was moody and on edge and ready to fight for the dumbest reason, especially if I caught you staring at me. I would ask, "What are you staring at?" with an attitude. *Coming from where I'm from, if you are staring you must have a problem and I was fitna solve it for you.* Yani did her best to keep me calm and let me know that I don't always have to get mad or be ready to fight everybody all the time. She would say, "Girl ain't nobody staring at you" and start laughing, which made me start laughing and chill. Thankfully, there weren't too many instances where I needed to snap at anyone, but I did curse a few people out for looking at me funny, though it was nothing major and didn't lead to a fight or anything to get me into trouble. Yani helped me loosen up a little bit because she was so silly and laughed at everything. Sometimes she would be a little too silly and get in trouble at school with our teacher, Mrs. Trisha. I don't know if Mrs. Trisha had it out for Yani, but it seemed like every time we laughed at something, every time we talked in class, Yani was the one to get caught and in trouble; *shockingly, I wasn't getting in trouble as much*. Yani was a talker during class, so she got in the most trouble with Mrs. Trisha. Mrs. Trisha used to make Yani stand in the corner with her face toward the wall and back facing the class. *I felt so bad for Yani.* I rarely saw her get upset with anyone, but I could tell she didn't like to be embarrassed by Mrs. Trisha, and I could tell she didn't like Mrs. Trisha, although it didn't stop Yani from being so goofy. As Yani and I went through the school year, I learned not to take everything so seriously, and our friendship continued to grow.

Yani and I began to hang out more at school and after school because we joined the volleyball team together. She joined the volleyball team first and talked me into joining, and I was hesitant, but I joined anyway. Surprisingly, Yani was good at volleyball. I found out later that her mother and her four sisters played volleyball, so volleyball was their family's sport, but I wasn't good at all. Listen, I will be the first to say it myself; *I sucked.* I couldn't hit the ball, serve the ball, or catch the ball to save my life. It took me a long time to get the hang of it, *like a season long.* Mr. Milburn, our coach, played me in the game, even when I sucked. I would miss ball after ball, and he would still play me because he wanted everyone on the team to get playing time. I actually didn't want as much play time as I got because I knew how bad I was, and I was scared every time I went in to play. I remember the last game of the season in 6th grade like it was yesterday. The game was tied at game point when Coach put me in the game to serve the last point. The pressure was real because if I missed the serve, we would lose the game, and if I made the serve, we had a fighting chance to win the game as long as we hit the ball back over the net. My mind started to race. I was so scared, but I really wanted to win this game, so I shook my nerves off and went for the serve. I served the ball right over the net and got an ace (a serve that the other team could not return)! We won the game off my serve! The whole team ran over to me cheering, hugging, and picking me up happy because we had won the game. I think they were happier that I sent the ball over the net. I was so happy with myself, and I felt good to be celebrated for the first time in my life by anyone. The celebration made me feel like I could do anything, and it made me want to continue to play volleyball. I felt like Yani and I had something in common now, and we would continue to be good friends.

Yani and I started to walk each other home and hang out more after school. She lived three minutes away from the school, so I would walk her home and then walk home by myself another twenty minutes to my house. Sometimes Yani would even walk me home and then walk home by herself, *which didn't make sense lol, b*ut that was what we did. One day when I walked her home from school, I got the chance to meet her family, and it was very interesting. I was standing outside waiting for Yani to come back out, and her mother, Ms. Linda came outside to say hi to me in her blouse and long denim skirt to her ankles, *right then and there I knew she was a church woman because only older church women wore denim skirts outside of the church.* "Hi Meena, you don't have to stand out here; you can come in!" she said in a loud voice, waving me into her house. When I walked into their house, I saw about seven or eight other children inside. There were five of Yani's sisters, about three or four foster children, and at that time, a house full of girls. Meeting Yani's family and seeing how happy and cared for they were made me wonder why my family couldn't be together and be a happy family. I wasn't jealous or anything; I just wanted to have a family of my own that was normal like Yani's. When Yani introduced me to her family, I was amazed at her mother, and at how she could take care of her own children and care for foster children like me, but not amazed enough to tell her or Yani I was a foster child myself.

I was afraid to tell anyone that I was a foster child, especially Yani because I was looking forward to building our friendship, a friendship I didn't want to be forced by pity. Even though Yani would have understood, I was too embarrassed to tell her that deep secret about me, so I kept it a secret for years. I was starting a new life, and I just couldn't add that part because I would have to go back in my past to explain the details. Yani was my friend, and I didn't want that to change because of my traumatic background. Her family was very lovely, as her sisters seemed to get along with each other. They weren't fighting or arguing with one another the way my sisters and I fought. The house was filled with regular conversations and happiness, something I didn't see growing up much in my own household with my family. Mrs. Linda was especially nice because she would take me out with them sometimes. She loved to drive and take day trips, and I would go along with them sometimes. While I was with Yani and her family, I was treated like family; everything Mrs. Linda did for her children, she did for me. The more I hung around Yani's family, the more I felt like a child of Mrs. Linda, even if I was just one of her foster children, because she treated them all the same.

Yani and I had been friends for years before we labeled our friendship status. There was no question whether we were friends or not; everyone knew that we were friends because we were always around each other. It wasn't until that one day in 9th grade when I was over Yani's house, and I was explaining how this other girl named Jade started telling people at school that I was her best friend. *For the record, this girl was never my best friend. Maybe I was her best friend, but she was not my best friend.* Jade was different. She was brown-skinned with hair longer than Yani, and she spoke very softly. Jade and I became friends and started hanging out together at school. She lived in a duplex about five minutes walking distance from the school. I walked Jade home a few times on my way home when I didn't walk with Yani and went into her house. Jade lived on the top floor of the duplex, but she told everyone she lived in a mansion. She tried to get me to lie and say that she lived in a mansion because I visited her house, but I didn't. Jade lied about a lot of things to make friends, like her mother and father were married and rich. It turned out her mother and father were divorced, living in different homes, and they were not rich. I had been to Jade's duplex with her father, and I had visited her mother's apartment on the other side of town. I only walked her home a few times because most of the time Yani and I walked home. At Yani's house, I was explaining to her while her sisters were around how Jade was telling people we were best friends, but I didn't want to be her best friend because she lied too much.

"Jade keeps telling people we are best friends, but I don't want to be her best friend," I told Yani and her sisters.

"I thought you and Yani were best friends because y'all are always together," Yani's older sister Evani commented.

I didn't know what to say, and I don't think Yani knew what to say either. We both looked at each other and said, "I guess we are best friends!" Since that day, we have claimed each other as best friends.

Most friendships break up due to lifestyle changes, disagreements, betrayal, distance, and many other reasons, but Yani and I never experienced anything that would end our friendship. We both respect, encourage, celebrate, and enjoy one another's presence. We've seen each other through almost every life experience since 6th grade and still presently from middle school to high school, through college and well into adulthood, children, marriage, and our spiritual journey.

Yani made my life a lot easier by having her as a best friend. She made me feel like I belong and I demonstrated how I am worth having a true friendship. We talked about almost everything and went just about everywhere together. She made me a better person, a calmer and nicer person. Yani and her family accepted me for who I was *or who I showed them I was* and made me feel comfortable enough to claim them as family. Our friendship was special then, and now, still to this very day. *Shout out to my Bestie and her family who claim me as their family!! Thank you, Bestie for being the best first example of true friendship. Friendship is not one-sided, but it goes both ways. I will meet you wherever, I love you Bestie!!* My new life was finally starting to set in for me in better ways, but the trauma from my past life wouldn't let me enjoy my new life.

In Memory of Evani. It's so sad that you had to leave us so soon, but you have been a beacon to so many people. So, I believe your work here is done. I thank you for upgrading me and Yani's friendship status from friends to best friends! Because of you, Yani and I have been Besties for the past 27 years and counting.

CHAPTER FIVE
THE PROMISE

I wanted to make new friends and make a different label for myself. After entering foster care, I vowed to myself that all the trouble-making nonsense would end and that I would not resort to fighting and getting suspended anymore. At all my other schools, I was labeled as the girl who's always fighting, the dirty kid, the bad kid, the girl who never had her hair done, the stinky kid, the ugly girl, etc. This time I wanted to be labeled as just a kid, or maybe a cool kid, *whatever that is.* So, I decided if I chilled, and didn't get in so much trouble, I would be alright. Truly, I am not a fighter. I didn't like to fight as much as I did when I was living with my mother, but I had to fight. *I had to protect myself against somebody,* and since I couldn't protect myself against my mother, protecting myself against other kids was my only option. It was the only way to let out the frustration that I had been holding on to daily. This time around it would be different. I wouldn't have anyone beating me every day for no reason; in fact, I wouldn't get beat at all because

I was being protected by the policies and procedures the government put in place for foster parents and children. So, to me, I could pull this no trouble-making, no fighting nonsense off. My foster parent kept me clean, I had new clothes and sneakers, and she kept my hair done, so my peers shouldn't have much to clown me for, so I thought I would be good. The school year started, and I was doing great. Yani and I were making new friends and having fun until I met this girl named Sienna.

Sienna was in my 6th-grade class at Shaw Middle School. *It wasn't my fault; Sienna kept coming for me y'all.* I knew I didn't like her, but that was not a reason for me to beat her up the way I did, but she wrote a check her ass couldn't cash. All school year long Sienna kept saying sly stuff to me like, "You ugly, your hair short" and other stupid stuff that would have gotten her block knocked off (punched in the face) a long time ago; *yo! I'm proud of myself. I went almost a whole school year without fighting. I did good.* She would look down at me like I was a peasant or something. Sienna was short, light-skinned, and thick but had a nicely shaped body, fully developed in all the right areas. She had to wear a C-cup bra, if not a D-cup, because she had big breasts, no stomach, and a butt that didn't make sense at our 12-year-old age. She was shaped like a Coca-Cola bottle, the boys would say. She had nice hair that was cut into a bob with the swoop in her face which she kept fingering behind her ear. She wasn't bad looking; *she reminded me of Tiny from Xscape before her surgeries, but a milder version*; however, Sienna's attitude was very ugly to me, and it was hard to see past the repugnance of her attitude, which added to her ugliness. Sienna had a mustache that made her lips look gross every time she put Vaseline on, and that's all she did was put Vaseline on all day. I guess she was trying to hide her mustache by making her lips super shiny. Sienna walked with a switch, always wore tight revealing clothes, and was fresh as hell being flirtatious with all the boys, and they flirted with her in return. She wasn't that bad looking, but to me, she was just a mean girl.

I hung out with my Yani and our mutual friend Sabria, whose best friend was Sienna. As you may be able to tell, I could care less about Sienna, but Sabria was cool. She was a little taller than Sienna and shorter than me. Sabria was brown skinned with long thick natural hair that went down past her shoulders. It was hard to tell (the shape of) Sabria's figure because she always wore baggy clothes at least two sizes too big; she seemed like a tomboy, I guess that was her style. She had a raspy voice and was very loud when she spoke and laughed. Most of the time when Yani and I would hang with Sabria, Sienna would be around, walking down the halls with us, sitting at the lunch table with us, and most of all, getting on my damn nerves. This one day we were all talking in a circle in science class about summer plans, and Sienna just kept staring at me with her face twisted up like she had a problem with me.

I finally asked her, "Why are you staring at me like that?"

She answered, "Girl, ain't nobody staring at your ugly ass!" Sienna's response echoed through the class because she thought she was going to embarrass me in front of everyone. She was wrong. The only thing I wanted to do was to whip that ass. Sienna kept going on and on talking about me, about how I dressed, my short hair, and stuff like that which didn't faze me. The class echoed, "Ooh, ahhhh, you gonna let her talk to you like that?" They wanted to see a fight, but I wanted to honor my commitment to the promise

I proclaimed to myself. *No fighting, and no getting suspended* kept playing in my mind until she finally blurted out, "I want to fight you!" *Well, that did it*, my commitment and promise went right out the window. I never backed down from a verbal challenge to fight. For some reason, I felt like I had something to prove, and I needed to do what I always wanted to do, which was whip that ass.

"Fine, we can fight, but after school though because I don't want to get suspended. Meet me outside right after school."

Yani looked at me and said, "Are you really going to fight her? We're all friends."

"I sure am. She talks too much. If I beat her up, then she will stop talking to me and leave me alone, and she is not my friend; she is you and Sabria's friend. I don't like her, never did, and probably never will."

"But can you fight?" Yani asked. She had never seen me fight before because of the promise I kept. Yani also didn't know how much I used to fight in my other schools. She had only met me this school year after I had wiped my own slate clean. When Yani and I first met, it wasn't exactly on my mind to tell her I *fought everyday at my other school, flushed some girls' heads down the toilet, and beat up some boys, got expelled from two schools before I met you, but now I am a saint.* Yani would have looked at me like I had two heads or something. See, Yani and I were cut from two completely different cloths. Her mother loved her and took good care of her by supplying her with the basic needs for living. Yani always had her hair done nicely, wore nice clean clothes, and was able to be herself around her mother. Her mother even had foster kids who lived with them, and she took great care of them, and treated them all as if they were her own. Yani's sisters got along with each other for the most part, but my life was different. I was a foster child; my mother didn't take good care of me, someone else did. My siblings and I weren't close; we were separated and alone in this world to fend for ourselves. I couldn't tell Yani about my life, I just had to show her, like I was showing myself, that I was a regular teenager of some sort. Even though I tried so hard to be a different person, and to make a new impression in my own life, I couldn't back down from this fight. This is the one actual fight I wanted to fight; I was going to fight.

"Show up, and you will see," I responded to Yani, nodding my head matter-of-factly.

"I got track practice; I will try and make it before practice, but it has to start right away, so I can see and make it to practice." she laughed, saying she could do both.

The day went on quickly and turned 3:00 p.m. on the dot. As soon as we were dismissed from class, I grabbed my things and started to head straight for the door. Everyone in the class was hyping everything up (instigating) and putting their bids on who was going to win the fight. Most of the kids bid on Sienna for some reason, but some bid on me. I heard "Oh, Tameena quiet, you gotta watch out for the quiet ones. They be the ones that can fight!" I didn't say a word. I've never been the one to trash talk; my mantra was, *I can show you better than I can tell you; okay I stole that mantra from my mother who said it before she beat me sometimes.* In any case, it was true, and I was ready to show her what I was made of, so she could leave me alone. I did not care about any bids; I was going to whip this girl's ass once and for all. Pushing through the loud crowd of students, excited to see a fight, I just walked straight out of the building and to our designated location. I waited for about 3 minutes before Sienna came out and it was theatrical. Sienna came walking out of the school with a posse of students with her. One girl had her bookbag, another held her purse, and Sienna had a small jar of Vaseline in her hand, the same jar she used to grease her lips. She dug her fingers into the jar scooping out a clump of Vaseline and began rubbing it into her hands and then onto her face. I didn't understand why she was putting it all over her face. I thought it was a light-skinned person thing because I saw my sister Isabella, who was light-skinned, do that before one of her fights. Later I learned that boxers use Vaseline to protect themselves during a fight, so when their opponents hit them, their faces would be too slippery for their hits to connect. When Sienna was done smothering her face, she walked to the corner sidewalk and I immediately got into my fighting stance with both fists balled up and to my face, with my power hand in front ready to blow. She swung the first hit at my face and I pulled back, her fist missing my face. Once I pushed my face back up and swung at her, I punched her straight in the nose. I didn't stop there, I continued to punch her, not caring where my punches landed. Sienna grabbed me by the hair, *a real girly girl move,* and started pulling it, trying to swing me around. I grabbed her hair with one hand and started punching her with the other. I was getting the best of her until she swung me around, and I tripped on the edge of the curb and we both tumbled straight to the ground. Sienna fell on top of me, but I rolled over on top of her, sitting on her torso and punching at her. Sienna blocked most of the hits to her face as she held her face in her arms. After a few hits, someone grabbed me and pulled me off her yelling, "Go, go, they coming!" talking about the school security officers. I got right off her and went on about my business like I was never in a fight and went home, so I didn't get caught and get in trouble.

Yani missed the whole fight because she went straight to track practice, but she heard about the fight the next day at school and questioned me about the details of the fight. I met Yani at her house, so we could walk to school together, and I began to tell her about the fight.

"Girl, what happened? I didn't know y'all was going to fight!" Yani asked.

"She was talking all this trash, and I meant what I said for her to meet me outside after school!" I said, whipping my hands back and forth.

"So, she actually met you outside, you actually went outside?!" Yani asked with her hands over her mouth.

"Girl- yes, how else were we gonna fight?"

"Ok, ok, ok, so who hit first?"

"Well, she swung first and missed, then I followed up with the boop, bop, shabang,"

"Wait, wait, wait, so when she tried to hit you, you ducked or did you like, move out of the way?"

"Um, I ducked I guess, it's the same thing as moving out of the way. I just know she swung at me and I dipped that jawn." I dipped my head down and came back up in my boxing stance.

"So, when you hit her, you actually had your hands like that?"

"Yeah girl, like ain't that's how you fight?" I asked while laughing at her questions.

"But was she like crying and stuff?"

"I don't know. I wasn't worrying about her crying. I was beating her up. Girl, you ask a lot of questions!"

We made it to school and when I reached my class, they were already talking about the fight. Sienna was in the class talking trash and laughing, "I beat her ass, you saw how I dropped her!" A different classmate chimed in, "No, you did not drop her. She tripped over the curb, and she beat your ass!" The class started laughing and Sienna sat looking salty (mad because she had lost, and everyone knew she lost). Sienna and I never became best friends or anything, but she respected me and left me alone, and I continued not to like her throughout the rest of middle school. For the next few weeks, I was "Tameena, the girl that beat Sienna's ass." That was the last physical fight I had gotten into throughout the rest of my life, but there were many close calls.

To be honest, when I made my promise, but my goal was not planned out well, I just planned on not fighting and not getting suspended. I didn't plan on curving my attitude. I didn't know how not to fight when being challenged, and I didn't plan on healing from the hurt of my past life with my mother. *Ok I did have therapy but didn't appreciate it that much. I'll explain later*. However, because I only got into one fight and had a few possible ones, *there were many possible ones* during my time in foster care and for the rest of my life, not fighting was a great accomplishment to me. Technically, I kept my truth. I pride myself on my ability to control my fits of rage, *at least to the point of* not *fighting someone*. Despite my promise, *I* was still definitely an angry person, but I felt accomplished with my one fight, the last fight I had throughout the rest of my childhood experience.

CHAPTER SIX
FAMILY ESTRANGEMENT

Lyfe was the next one to leave Grandma's house. She ran away and decided to "live with her fr-fr-friends in the streets'' as my grandma would say. None of Lyfe's friends were good to be around, all they did was start trouble, stay out all night smoking, and drinking their lives away. It was all happening way too fast; first, Sophie left to go live with my mother, then Lyfe left Fifi and me for the streets, and leaving us to fend for ourselves. I knew it was only a matter of time before Fifi would also leave me to go be with Lyfe; they were inseparable. Although Fifi copied everything Lfye did, she was smarter than Lyfe because she didn't leave Grandma's right away. She tried to talk some sense into Lyfe before she left, but it was unsuccessful.

It all started when Lyfe would hang out late — coming in at all times of the night. She was coming home at midnight, 1 a.m., 2 a.m. It became later and later until she started to stay out for nights at a time. Grandma would warn and threaten Lyfe that she was going to change the locks and not let her back in the house if she kept coming in late. One day Fifi and I were in our room getting dressed, and Grandma was sitting downstairs in the living room watching TV.

Lyfe had been gone for two days before she stormed into the house high and drunk, yelling at Grandma and slurring, "I'm leaving this house. You don't have to worry about me no more. You happy now; I will be out of your gray ass hair."
Fifi and I rushed to put the rest of our clothes on to run downstairs and see what was happening.

"W-w-wait just one m-m-miniute. Where h-have you b-b-been Lyfe?" Grandma asked.

Lyfe mocked Grandma, answering, "I b-b-bb-b-been out, and I'm getting my stuff and leaving and not coming back!"
Lyfe flew past Fifi and me on the steps and ran upstairs to pack her stuff; Fifi and I followed her trail.

"Lyfe, where are you going?" I asked her.

"Yeah, you don't have anywhere to live, where will you go"? Fifi asked.

76

Lyfe responded, "Don't worry about it. Y'all can stay here if you want to, but I'm going," she said, gathering her things then racing down the stairs and running straight out the door. It was so quick — Lyfe grabbed a bag and was gone with no detailed explanation to anyone; she was just gone. I couldn't believe she would just up and leave us like that, especially because she was the older sister. *I don't know why I thought any differently because I was the real big sister.* Grandma went out the front door yelling "Lyfe, come b-b-back here!" but Lyfe never even turned around, and just like that, it was just Fifi and I living with Grandma.

I've seen Lyfe run away from my mother before, and she always came back home, so I kind of expected her to come back to Grandma's house, which she did, but not to live; it was only to visit. After Lyfe ran away, our lives were changing again. Fifi started to hang out more and I had no idea where she was going. We had different sets of friends; I hung out with my neighbors across the street or I hung out with Yani. I didn't know who Fifi hung around because I was gone off doing my own thing. Fifi hung out and would sometimes come back home drunk, sometimes high, and sometimes drunk and high. One day, it dawned on me that Fifi was linking up with Lyfe daily. Just like Lyfe, Fifi started to hang out until the wee hours of the morning, and Grandma would give her the same spiel she gave Lyfe. "I'm gonna ch-ch-change the locks on you one d-d-day and you w-w-won't be able to g-g-get back in my house," Grandma would say. Fifi would respond, "Well do it!" and go on about her business. It wasn't until I started seeing Lyfe lurking around the block asking Fifi to bring her some food and water. I had finally confirmed it — Fifi was hanging around with Lyfe.

Every time I saw Lyfe she looked like she was hooked on drugs, and I did not know what to say or do, so I didn't do anything. I looked the other way or walked in the other direction whenever I saw her around the block. One day I was in the house alone while Grandma was at one of her appointments when Fifi came into the house and started packing a plastic grocery store bag with food and water.

"What are you doing — are you running away too?" I asked with an attitude.

"No, I'm giving some food to Lyfe because she is hungry," Fifi answered without looking at me.

"Why don't you tell her to come back home? I'm sure Grandma will let her back in!" I said.

"She not coming back here, and that lady only cares about you. She don't care about Lyfe or me!" Fifi answered fiercely.

"Why does everyone keep saying that? She is taking care of all of us, but Lyfe and now you keep acting up. She don't have to put up with this, but she does!" I said agitated.

Fifi answered, "Well, I guess we will see."

Then Fifi walked out of the house to meet up with Lyfe and gave her the bag. Fifi continued to hang out with Lyfe and steal food for her for a while until Lyfe started going against Fifi.

Lyfe was the only friend Fifi had and oftentimes they were more like best frenemies for some reason. One minute they were hanging out with each other, and the next they were fighting each other verbally and physically. I could always tell when Fifi and Lyfe were not getting along because Fifi would come home cussing and fussing with an attitude about what Lyfe did or she would just be home for a few days, without going out. On this one particular day, Fifi and I were home during one of their disagreements, and Grandma was sitting outside on the porch. Lyfe walked up to the house with two girls and made all this noise, calling out from the bottom of the steps, "Fifi, Fifi, get yo' ass out here."

I came outside to see Grandma telling Lyfe to go away and Lyfe went off saying "No, she needs to come out here, we're gonna whip her ass!"

Lyfe and the two girls had their heads wrapped up with scarves and had sweatpants on looking ready to fight.

I stood at the top of the steps yelling at Lyfe, "You think you gonna come here with some girls to jump my sister, you must be out of your fucking mind!"

Lyfe went on to plead her case, "She stole money from me and I know she did it because I showed her where I keep my money, and now it's gone. She's either gonna give me my money or we fighting!"

To that, I replied, "Ok, but you not finna jump my sister with some girls. How you gonna bring other girls to fight your own sister?

You fucking crackhead. I will beat you and your friends the fuck up!"

Fifi came yelling from behind the screen door, "I didn't take your money. Why are you blaming me? You need to be checking your girls!"

I yelled back. "Stay in the house, Fifi! She not gonna touch you; none of them are!"

Grandma was trying to get a word in saying "Ta-m-m-meena, get back in the house and c-c-close the door!"

I listened and went into the house, straight to the kitchen to grab a knife, and walked myself right back outside. Lyfe and her friends were still at the bottom step talking trash, banging their fists together ready to fight. When I came out with my knife, Grandma was scared, yelling for me to go inside.

She kept yelling "That's your s-s-sister, that's your sister, go on now b-b-back in the house!"

I refused Grandma's demand and yelled "Lyfe, I swear to God, I will kill you right where you stand if you don't get from the front of this house!"

"You ain't gonna do shit!" she responded, attempting to move up the steps.

There were only four steps that led to the porch. She and her friends moved up to the third step and I moved down to the second step with my knife pointing at Lyfe's chest; I did not hesitate before kicking her down the stairs. Lyfe and her friends went tumbling down two steps falling onto the concrete.

"I swear I better not see none of y'all around here again because I will whip y'all asses, and Lyfe, I will fucking kill you; I never liked yo' ass anyway!"

Lyfe and her friends got up off the ground and walked away talking trash, saying "We be back!"

"You better hope you don't," I said, swaying my knife back and forth as they left.

Grandma was on the porch staring at me like I was crazy; slowly taking the knife out of my hand and leading me into the house and closing and locking the door behind us. She had never seen me behave in such a way and was probably rethinking if she wanted to keep fostering me; *lol, shoot I was rethinking it for her.* Despite everything that happened that day, a few days later Fifi and Lyfe were best friends again, and I wound up in a therapist's office.

Grandma was worried about me after pulling a knife out and kicking Lyfe and friends down a few stairs. She spoke to my social worker at the time and explained that I needed counseling to let out the anger I had inside of me. About a week later my Grandmom and I had a serious conversation.

"Tameena, you sc-sc-scared me the other day when you p-p-pulled out a knife. Were you re-re-really going to st-st-stab your sister? Grandma asked.

"Grandmom, I'm sorry I scared you. I don't know what I was going to do; I just knew I wasn't going to let Lyfe jump my sister," I explained.

"I sp-sp-spoke to your so-so-social worker, and we think you sh-sh-should see a counselor to h-h-help you control your anger when you are upset, be-be-because you just can't g-g-go around pulling a knife on p-p-people," Grandma warned.

"I don't want to go to counseling, but I will go if you think it will help," I answered.

I started counseling the next week and I hated it every bit, because she asked me the same questions repeatedly, "How does this make you feel, what are you feeling now, why do you think you responded the way you responded?" I would say things like "How you think I feel? Angry, of course, because that's why I'm here," with an attitude. Most of the time I did not participate, I just sat there until the end of our session; meanwhile, Fifi was out living her best life with Lyfe.

More and more, Fifi started to hang out with Lyfe and even started staying out overnight — until one night Fifi left for the last time, taking a bag of clothes with her repeating the cycle of Lyfe. I didn't try to stop her. *I'd like to think because I knew I couldn't stop her.* She was Lyfe 2.0 and the only friend she had and they *had* to be together. Just like that, I was estranged from all my family members in less than a year. As far as I was concerned, Lyfe and Fifi fell off the face of the earth because I didn't see them again after they ran away. Although I was used to the feeling of abandonment, it hurt to know that I was officially alone in this world and this made me act out at home. I started to have mental breakdowns where I would be so depressed that I didn't listen to anything Grandma asked of me. Sometimes I would just break out in tears, or I would break out in a fit of rage trashing my room, yelling, and screaming. Most of the time my fits of rage happened when I was alone, but a few times they happened while my grandma was home. Grandma did not know what to do with me; she simply watched me break down and was there for me when I came out of it, but I know this was too much for her to handle at the age of 65. After a few times, Grandma took me back to a therapist to help me talk through my trauma, but I rarely spoke during my sessions.

CHAPTER SEVEN
RESPITE CARE

Growing up in foster care has always left me feeling estranged from the world and the people around me. In many ways, there were expressions or indications that constantly reminded me that I wasn't truly a part of any group or family. I had been given labels, treated differently, pushed around, and taken advantage of.

No matter how well I was being treated or how attached I became to my foster families and others that took me in, the label "foster" made me feel disconnected from everyone. The label "foster" was often combined with familial terms such as "foster daughter," "foster niece," "foster granddaughter," and my least favorite was, "foster child." To me, this only made the term feel less endearing. It only reinforced that I didn't belong and that the people who brought me into this world didn't want me. This was a feeling that stayed with me, not only throughout my time in foster care but beyond. It caused an inescapable sense of loneliness, even in a room full of people who at least cared enough to take me in. I lived with my foster grandmother for four years; we had a great relationship, and she treated me well. To me, she was my grandma, but to her, I was her "foster child." Regardless of how long I stayed with a family — whether it was for one day, one year, or four years- the label "foster" still preceded our relationship, thus defining me. I often wondered if the label "foster" carried with it the potential for mistreatment by some who took me in.

As an educator working with foster care students, I understand that not all foster families mistreat their foster children. However, as a former foster child myself, I have firsthand experience of some foster families mistreating their foster children. My foster grandmother did not mistreat me herself; she may have neglected to notice that I was being raped by her son later, but she herself did not mistreat me. Grandma always tried to include me, but there was this one-time Grandma could not take me on vacation. The vacation was pre-planned before I was placed in her home. That summer, for one week, she placed me in Respite Care.

Respite Care is an arrangement system where another foster family takes you in, for a certain amount of time, until your foster family is able to take you back. *It's like a formalized babysitting club of "trained professional" backup foster parents.* It was my first time in respite care, and I was already anxious about being away from my foster home. Even though Grandma had prepared me ahead of time that I would be staying with a different family for a week until she returned from Florida, I was devastated at the thought of living with another stranger, even if it was only for a week. At the time, I had never been to Florida and wanted to go so badly, but I guess I wasn't family enough to take family vacations with Grandma just yet. To help ease my worries about staying with another family, my grandma took me to the Gallery to buy new clothes, shoes, and a suitcase for packing my things. The Gallery was located on 11th and Market Street in downtown Philly; we caught the #34 trolley two blocks away from our house. I was filled with excitement as I sat next to Grandma holding her soft hand. It didn't take long to get to the Gallery, only about 20 minutes. When we arrived, I was amazed at all the stores that circled around me. I had never been in a place that had so many different stores to shop at, and it also had restaurants to eat at in one place; *this is vacation,* I thought. We shopped around, and I bought five new outfits, one pair of white low-top Reebok sneakers, and a pretty pink suitcase from JCPenney. After we shopped, we stopped at a Chinese store in the food court to eat lunch, and for dessert, we ate at Cinnabon, which became one of my favorite desserts. We traveled back to the house before the sun fell, and Grandmom and I packed my suitcase for the next day, the day I would be handed over to another family. Although my grandma made me feel like I was going on vacation too, she did not know that she was sending me into a living nightmare.

My social worker picked me up the next day to transport me to my new family for the week. Everything looked good when we got there, and from what I could see downstairs, the house was cleaned, and the family looked normal. There was a mother and father named Mr. and Mrs. Wilkins and their two biological children, Tyler, and Jessica. The parents seemed a little younger than my grandmother but still old enough to be my grandparents, and the children were close to my age. Their son Tyler was 16, and their daughter Jessica was 12; the same age as me. The two of them introduced themselves after their parents, and I introduced myself to them before Jessica took me to the room where I would be sleeping. On the way to the room, Jessica gave me a tour upstairs. It was a three-bedroom house, which was smaller than my grandma's four-bedroom house. When we reached the top of the stairs, the bathroom was right in front of us. Next to the bathroom was Mr. and Mrs. Wilkins's bedroom, the middle bedroom where Tyler slept, and then Jessica's room in the back where I would sleep in her extra twin bed. The rooms looked normal, but the bathroom stuck out to me. The bathroom was clean, but everything seemed permanently stained. When I walked into the bathroom, I saw a sink directly in front of me. The basin on the sink had cracks and rust lines in between. To the left of the sink was the toilet, which also had tears in its soft cushion seat. I could tell the cushion was originally white, but the color had faded in some parts to a darker tan, and the tears were darker and dirtier. I didn't want to sit on the toilet when I needed to go to the bathroom, but I did anyway. Even though the cushion was soft, the tears in the cushion scratched and pinched my skin. *I remember to this day the pinches I got when I sat on that toilet.* Next to the toilet were the tub and shower. The tub had chipped paint and a rusty look around the drain. The faucet was stainless steel, *more like stainful steel* that was stained with black marks on the spout. The walls around the bathroom were covered with wallpaper, painted tan. Pieces of the wallpaper were hanging from the walls, making the bathroom look like it was falling apart. For some reason, the wall around the water pipes was missing; all I could see was the spout and the water pipes connected to something somehow- an open space behind it with a little closed door that led to Mr. and Mrs. Wilkins's room. It looked like maybe the bathroom was being remodeled, starting with the tub, even though water still ran from the spout. I moved on to Jessica's pretty pink room with pink walls, pink dresser drawers, and two pink bed frames with pink sheets on each bed. I left my suitcase closed in a corner of the room and sat on the bed that Jessica pointed out to me.

Jessica was nice; she let me play with her dolls and dollhouse. I had never had a doll or doll house before. Even though we may have been a little too old for dolls, I enjoyed playing with her while we were in her room. Tyler was cool too. He stayed in his room most of the time. Sometimes we would go outside and play with the other kids, but I mostly sat on the step and watched Tyler and Jessica play. The first night, after playing outside Mrs. Wilkins called out for us to come into the house.

"Tyler, Jessica, and uh, um, you child, come on in to eat dinner!" she yelled from inside the house.

"Okay, Mom!" Tyler and Jessica responded in unison.

I just followed behind them and got ready for dinner. While Mrs. Wilkins was making dinner plates, Tyler, Jessica, and I sat at the dinner table with Mr. Wilkins. The table was about 6 ft long and 4 ft wide. Mr. Wilkins sat at the head of the table with Jessica seated next to him on the side, while I sat next to her on the other side. Mrs. Wilkins sat at the other end of the table, and Tyler sat along the other long side of the table. When Mrs. Wilkins served the plates, she served Mr. Wilkins first, next Jessica, skipped me and served Tyler, sat her plate of food in front of her empty seat, and finally served me last. It bothered me a little when she skipped over me, but then I thought I was being emotional. *Why did she skip over me and feed me last, like she was gonna run out of food or something? Nah, I'm trippin; she is not used to me being here,* I thought as I quickly

93

removed the thought from my mind, only to be right. Every meal I ate for my entire stay, I was served last, even if I was in the first seat. This made me feel alone and unwanted; like I didn't belong. *I only need to be here for a few days,* I thought to myself every day during meals. Even when Jessica and I would play with Jessica's toys, Mrs. Wilkins was always checking on us, telling me to be careful with Jessica's things. One day Jessica and I were coloring; and Jessica only had one coloring book, but we both wanted to color in it at the same time. We were having a coloring contest to see who colored the neatest. Since there was only one coloring book and we wanted to color different pages, I asked Jessica if it was okay that I rip out a page so we both could color. Jessica said yes, and I ripped out one coloring sheet that I would color so Jessica could color in her book. Mrs. Wilkins walked into the room to check on us again and snapped out on me because I had ripped a page out of the coloring book.

"Why would you rip a page out of my daughter's book?" Mrs. Wilkins yelled.

"I'm sorry, she said I could so we could both color!" I responded with a huge ball in my throat.

94

"You can't just go around destroying other people's things like that! You should have asked me!" Mrs. Wilkins aggressively said as she snatched the paper from under my hand.

"You are not allowed to touch her things for the rest of the time that you are here!" she snarled.

It's a fucking coloring book, I thought in my head. I expected Jessica to pass me an assist here and tell her mother that she let me rip the paper out, but she never said a word. I was so upset, but I was not on my home turf, so I swallowed my frustration and stayed to myself.

Mr. Wilkins didn't do much but work and sleep. When he came home from work, he greeted Jessica with a kiss, and Tyler with a pound, but said absolutely nothing to me; he didn't even so much as look at me. I understood that I wasn't his child, but *I didn't ask you to take me into your home; shit, take me back,* I wanted to blurt out. He treated me as if I were imposing on his family time, which I probably was, but again, *I didn't ask to be here.* Sometimes Mr. and Mrs. Wilkins would be up in their bedroom while Tyler, Jessica, and I were downstairs; he would call down to Tyler and Jessica. They would run upstairs to him, and they would be in his room for about 30 minutes to an hour without calling for me. When they came down, they would tell me that they were watching TV in their parents' room with their parents. They left me alone downstairs to have a movie night upstairs amongst themselves and did not invite me. I became uncomfortable and irritable, wanting so badly to go home, for I knew I was not welcomed, and things were getting very weirder.

One day, I thought I would get up early to take a shower. The plan was to get in and out of the shower before everyone else got up so that I wouldn't be in anyone's way. I got out of bed, grabbed my clothes, walked to the bathroom, and got into the shower. I let the water run on me for a quick second and then began to close my eyes while I washed my face. For some reason, I felt weird, like I was being watched or something. I was facing the shower spout with my face in the water to rinse the soap off and then turned around to start washing the rest of my body. When I was all done washing my body, I turned around to rinse myself off and looked down when I saw a pair of eyes looking at me. I jumped back and almost slipped backward, trying to keep my feet from slipping in front of me, and caught myself. Then I looked again to see if my eyes were playing tricks on me. I looked down again and saw Mr. Wilkins peering through the little door from his bedroom into the hole in the wall in the bathroom. I let out an *Oh my God* as I jumped back again, so afraid of what to do or say. To my startle, Mr. Wilkins jumped, bumping his head in that small space, trying to get his head out of the little door. I quickly jumped out of the tub, not fully rinsed off, and went to make sure the bathroom door was locked, because I was afraid he would try to come into the bathroom with me. The bathroom door was locked, and I wrapped my towel around myself and sat on the toilet, silently crying with my face in my hands and on my knees. There was a knock at the bathroom door, but I didn't attempt to answer or open it; I sat there silently, barely taking any breaths. I did not know what to do. *Should I scream, should I answer the door, or should I just sit here?* I thought. I decided to sit there and not say a word. It felt like the bathroom's blistered walls were caving in on me as if they were going to fall apart. Mr. Wilkins knocked on the door a few times before Mrs. Wilkins woke up and walked out of her bedroom to go to the bathroom. Mrs. Wilkins saw her husband knocking on the bathroom door, and he said, "I think the girl is in the shower. Tell her to hurry out so I can use the bathroom."

"Hey, girl, hurry out the shower; don't use all the hot water!" Mrs. Wilkins instructed.

"Okay, coming out in a minute," I muttered in a shaky voice, relieved to hear any voice other than Mr. Wilkins'. I was so afraid that my bare body shook in fear. I quickly put all my clothes on, opened the door, and rushed out of the bathroom and into Jessica's room, and got back in bed. I went under the covers, afraid to do anything else. *I can't wait to get back to my grandma's house. It's crazy over here*, I said to myself under the covers. I kept what I saw to myself because I didn't want to disrupt the happiness of their home. Also, I didn't think anyone would believe me; I was just a foster child, not even their foster child — *a foster child of another foster parent.* Besides, if it's one thing that I know how to do, I know how to conceal and cut off my feelings. I made sure to not make eye contact with Mr. Wilkins and to never be caught alone with him for

1) to help me with the process of concealing, and 2) just in case he tried to take advantage of me inappropriately. I tried to stay away from everyone in the house as much as possible for the next two days, by neglecting the shower, and only leaving the bed for meals until my social worker came back to pick me up. When my social worker picked me up, we greeted each other, and I rode silently in the back seat of her car for the rest of the ride until we reached home. I was so glad to see Grandma, but I was so upset that she left me with those people.

CHAPTER EIGHT
THE NIGHT CREEPER

I woke up in the middle of the night to someone in my bottom bunk bed with me. The bunk bed was against the wall to the right of the room. My back was turned toward my room door so I didn't see, hear, or feel who came into my room and into my bed. Now if anyone knows me, they know I love to sleep, and I am a heavy sleeper, at least I used to be a heavy sleeper. After this encounter, I barely went to sleep. I was awakened out of my sleep by physical and verbal threats by someone who was a really close person to me. When I discovered who it was behind me, I was disappointed, confused, scared, and embarrassed.

Prior to this, this person was fun to be around. He gave me gifts, took my sisters and me to his house, and he usually had lots of snacks and candy. It was always so much fun when my sisters Lyfe, Phoenix and I would go over to his house to have a good time with his children. He had three children: one boy and two girls. Every time we went over, he would pick us up in his gray two-door Celica.

My three sisters would sit in the back seat, and I always sat in the front seat. I lived in Southwest Philly, but he lived in South Philly in the Passyunk Projects. It was about a 15-minute drive from my house. On the drive, we would talk and listen to music, and it was fun for me because it was different when I was living with my mother. It was better, and it was safer, but it was all too good to be true because I was definitely not safe.

This person visited Grandma every day, but my sisters and I would go visit him on the weekends. We wouldn't stay the night or anything; we would just go on Saturdays and stay the day because we had to go to church on Sunday morning with Grandma (we never missed church). It was so fun. We would get to his place and run through the projects with his children and the other children from there. There were so many different sections and buildings in the projects. The buildings were just about eight feet tall and eight feet wide, with about six or seven different buildings in each section. Each section was named a different Terrace and the buildings were separated by small lawns and concrete walkways. I remember there was this big dirty mattress in the back of the projects we used to jump on and do flips. *I just realized how nasty that was back then, but it was so much fun!* Sometimes we would race between the houses, jump rope, play basketball, and so many other games that we probably made up on our own. We were in the projects so, of course, I witnessed some fights there. One fight was with his daughter Jody. She ran out of the house with a sock full of batteries ready to fight. *I ain't never seen anything like that before — somebody just running around with a sock of batteries to fight.* Lyfe and Sophie would get into fights when we went over there too, *I guess it reminded them of our old neighborhood in North Philly,* but this fight was crazy. Jody ran past everyone in the house cussing and fussing about how she was going to beat this girl up. Lfye, Fifi, and I followed behind her all the way into Pepper Terrace (another building in the projects). Jody ran up to the girl while she was standing with her friends and just started whacking her with the sock of batteries. The girls' friends tried to jump in it, but Lyfe, Fifi, and I started knuckling up with the friends. I don't even know how the fight ended, but I know that Jody had a bloody sock of batteries in her hand; the girl she fought was messed up. She had gashes, whelps, and bruises all over her face. It was horrifying to me because I had never seen nor been in a fight that bad before, *if I don't count my mother's beatings, they used to be brutal*. I didn't know people would hurt someone so bad the way Jody hurt this girl, *I guess it was a South Philly Thing.* Otherwise, Jody was a good person and fun to be around, but after that fight, I stayed out of her way. Other than the fight, we had some good times over at this person's house. After a while, he wanted me to come over to his house without Lyfe and Fifi. He would blame it on how misbehaved they were (they were misbehaving a lot), and how much they got in trouble (they did get into a lot of trouble). I was the "good one" — that's what most people said about me. Everyone loved me because I wasn't a "troubled child." So, there were times when I rode with him alone without my sisters, and that's when things got weird.

The first few times I rode with this person alone, we just listened to music. He would be driving, but side-eyeing me every once in a while, with a puzzled look on his face, as if he was trying to figure me out. The ride wasn't long so we got to his place rather quickly before the weirdness started. As the ride continued, I started to get more uncomfortable with him because of the dirty looks, the things he would say to me, and eventually the bad touches. He would say things like, "What's up, cutie," and honestly, when he first started calling me that, I didn't think anything of it. I was 12 and didn't think he thought I was cute; as far as I was concerned, it was a term of endearment. Until one day I rode in the car with the oldest son alone to his house because my other sisters did not want to go. I always wanted to go out and have fun. There were times he would stick his tongue out at me. I thought he was being funny, and I would stick my tongue out back at him jokingly. *Man, I was so naive.* One day, I stuck my tongue out at him and he said, "Alright, I will show you what to do with that tongue." He said it in a whisper so I could get closer to him and ask him what he said, so he could nudge me away but by touching me in inappropriate places. Sometimes he would nudge me away with his hands on my chest, (which I didn't think anything of at first, probably because I was flat as a pancake). Sometimes he would nudge me away by putting both hands on my shoulders, turning me around, and pushing me away with his hands on my waist. One day he visited Grandma's house and brought some toys. I said, "I like it, thank you," and he whispered, "You like that, huh? I got something else you would like!" *Uggh, this is so hard to write without feeling disgusted.* He nodded his head up and down with his left arm across his stomach and his right hand on his chin, and his tongue rested between his teeth in the top row of his mouth. *This man was 46 years old at the time but was missing his two front teeth at the top of his mouth looking like a toddler.* His tongue curled up through the gap between his teeth and the tip of his tongue touched his top lip, and it looked truly disgusting. Whenever he made this look, I knew he was thinking something nasty. Meanwhile, at this point all the fresh and inappropriate remarks, and disgusting gestures were never followed up with anything seemingly inappropriate to anyone else, so I didn't express to anyone my disgust and annoyance.

Well, on this one night, everything changed. It was in the middle of the night when I was awakened from my sleep. I was lying on my right side facing the wall in my room. His body covered me like the bun to a hotdog I once saw him devour. This man took one bite of the hotdog and only had the end of the bread part left. The hotdog didn't have a chance and neither did I as I tried to get out of his grip. He was a thick man and had me in a bear hug from behind. I could tell by the weight of his arms around me and the smell of his body, who it was behind me. I tried to turn around to see so I could know for sure who was behind me and what was happening, but he put his hand around my mouth still trying to force his privates into me and eventually succeeding. I felt something hard pushing against my vagina. I put my hands between my legs to separate my legs from his and touch where the pain was as I tried to ease the pain. There was something there between my legs touching my vagina; it was a penis, a man's big hard penis. He had his pants down, and my pants, too. I started to groan and cry because of the pain I felt and the restraints against me. At this time, he had a hand on my mouth and the other arm under my body wrapping around my waist to keep me close. My left arm was pushing against his waist and my right arm was squished to my right side because of his arm around me. I found out exactly who was behind me when he held my mouth tighter and told me to shut up and be quiet. It was then that I recognized his voice — it was Uncle P. I knew by the lisp he had from the huge gap between his front teeth. *Why would he do this to me?* I thought in my head. I screamed in pain but my screams were quieted by the force of his huge hand across my mouth. Despite the pain, knowing who it was I couldn't keep still as I wiggled and squirmed the entire time, he was behind me. He just held me tighter pushing in and out, in and out of me, as he breathed heavily, panting like a dog. When he was finished, he stopped pushing against my vagina but stayed in it. He rested his head on the back of my neck for a few seconds as his nasty, smelly sweat dripped on me. He came out of my vagina but still held me tight as if I were his long-lost love. I felt hurt, and I felt like what just happened didn't feel good and it wasn't right. Before he got out of my bed he whispered in my ear, "Don't scream and if you ever tell anyone I will kill you and your sisters." At this time, I was the only one living there; my sisters were gone. Sophie went back to live with my mother; Lyfe and Fifi were taken away and put into group homes. Therefore, I didn't understand how he was going to kill them, but I didn't want to test his threat, so I did as he said. I kept my mouth shut and suffered in silence just as I did back home with my mother. As he got out of bed, I was too scared to turn around. When I finally got the nerve to turn around, he was standing at the door with his back facing me, fiddling with his pants. I noticed his build from behind. He sounded like Uncle P, and from the silhouette of him in my dark room, he stood like Uncle P; therefore, in my mind, it was Uncle P, but I didn't see his face. I knew for sure he was him. I said "Uncle P" but he never turned around, yet he felt the need to remind me before he left, "If you say anything, I will kill you and your sisters, and by the way, I know where Lyfe and Fifi is, so don't try to be smart," as he finished fixing himself with his back still toward me, and walked sideways, careful not to show his face while exiting my room. I wanted to get up, I wanted to yell for help, but I was so afraid I never left the bed until the next morning.

It was hard for me to grasp the pain I was feeling physically along with the fact that my Uncle P did this to me. The night was long and I couldn't go back to sleep right away; I attempted to smell and feel on the green sheet (my comfort blanket) I brought from my home which normally helps calm me down and get to sleep, but Uncle P's scent was on my sheet and I couldn't bear the smell of it, so I threw it off my bed. I cried in pain and fear — fear of threats and fear of not knowing why he would do this to me and why I couldn't tell anyone. I thought, *who would I tell? Would they believe me? I'm a foster child, a bad child, a troubled child; no one would believe me.* What I was experiencing was different for starters. The pain I was feeling was something different; it wasn't like the guys on the block when I was living with my mother who touched me with their fingers, and their little penises. The aftermath of this was way more painful. I wanted to fall asleep because maybe the pain would go away and perhaps, I would feel better in the morning, maybe it was a horrible nightmare and none of this really happened. Sadly, morning came, and I didn't feel better. I was very sore between my legs, my vagina was sore, my legs were weak, and I just felt like a ton of bricks fell on me. I got up and tip-toed in pain to the bathroom and noticed that my underwear was a little messy. Messy like a bloody mess. I wasn't sure what it was from because I already had my period for the month. I was so embarrassed with myself; I just threw my underwear away. As I was in the bathroom, I prayed for God to help me as I slid down the bathroom door in tears. Deep down inside I knew what happened but couldn't believe it. I knew that Uncle P had sex with me. I knew I had to get off the floor and shower. Although I was in pain, my vagina was throbbing like it had a heartbeat of its own. I knew at some point I had to get up and shake it off. I peeled myself off the floor, reached for the shower, turned it on, got in, and cleaned myself off as I watched the blood run down my legs, like a murder scene from a TV show.

That day Uncle P didn't come over to visit Grandma. *I know it was him*, I thought, *who else would get in without breaking the door down unless someone had a key*? Grandma locked her door every night before bed unless she forgot this day and a complete stranger just walked in the house and came straight up to my room. Something just didn't feel or seem right about this story. I wanted so much to tell Grandma, but my mind was entangled in contemplation about how the conversation would unfold. *Where would I go? Who will take care of me and love me the way Grandma does? I don't want to go to another foster home, and I don't want to go back to my mom's house to get beat on. I don't want my sisters or myself to die. God help me.* About six months earlier, Fifi was taken away because she accused Uncle P of raping her. Grandma didn't believe her, and the social worker didn't believe her either because Fifi was "a bad child." To everyone, they were just troubled teenagers who would grow to be a statistic in the system. At the time of the accusations, Uncle P had never touched me so I didn't know if it was the truth; I just knew he never touched me. Grandma had already gone through enough around that time, and I just couldn't do that to her again; it would break her heart. I didn't want to tell anyone because no one would believe me either, or then I would be looked at as a statistic in the system, as well. I had been through multiple social workers and did not feel comfortable enough to express what I was experiencing. Besides, I know this may sound crazy, but I was happy where I lived because I didn't get beat on, I got nice clothes and sneakers, and I loved Grandma and she loved me. I was Grandma's favorite. I couldn't break her heart for her to hate me and send me away like she sent Lyfe and Fifi away, never knowing what the rest of my life would be like after leaving. As a result, I stayed in my room all day. I felt embarrassed and like I brought this on myself. *Were my clothes too revealing? Did I play too much?* were some of the many things I thought and blamed on myself. There was no way I could tell anyone about this situation.

Uncle P came by the house a few days later while I was lying in my bed. Grandma was sitting downstairs in the living room watching television. I heard him say, "Hey mama." When I heard that, every bone and feeling in my body dropped in pain and shame. I stayed in my room; I couldn't even stand to see him again. Of course, he had to go to the bathroom. I heard his footsteps as he walked up the steps and went into the bathroom. I listened as I was on my bed to see if he would sneak his way into my room again. My room is next to the bathroom, so it would just be my luck for him to pay me a visit. I buried my head into the bed because if he had decided to walk into my room, I didn't want to see him. The next thing I know, I hear the bathroom door open and about three steps to my bedroom door. My heart began to beat faster and faster as I lay in bed. Uncle opened my bedroom door and peeked in. I pretended as if I were asleep, and then he walked back out. So many thoughts crossed my mind as I asked myself, *why would you pretend to be asleep when you know he likes it when you're sleeping? Big dummy, he raped you in your sleep.* However, I didn't know what to do or how to react. My main focus was to not make contact with him until I was ready. The pain of what Uncle P did to me was still fresh and bothering my very being. Uncle P walked down the stairs and talked to Grandma for a while; I just stayed in my bed and cried. I wrote in my journal everything that happened to me a few nights before. I must have written about seven pages front and back describing every little detail and every feeling. I knew if I couldn't tell anyone, I could at least write about it and let it out lyrically so I could still live here and be loved by Grandma but knowing that I would have to face him one day.

Uncle P started to come around daily again, and I would do my best to stay out of his way, but somehow, he always found a way to get close to me. One day, I was in the kitchen making myself a bowl of cereal. Grandma was sitting on the front porch enjoying the nice summer weather. Uncle P walked into the kitchen and stuck his tongue out at me, but I didn't stick my tongue back out at him this time. I attempted to pass him so I could leave the kitchen. He grabbed me and kissed me on my mouth and neck, grabbed my butt, picked me up, and sat me on the countertop. It was so disgusting to me, *eww, the smell of him still haunts me as I write these words. It gives me dry heaves and shivers to this day.* At first, I moved my face and tightened my neck because it felt weird, and the smell of saliva was making me sick. He was facing me, staring me dead in the face like I was his lover. I didn't do anything. I didn't even look at him; I just sat there avoiding eye contact. He started to touch me in different places on my body, specifically between my legs. He then unzipped my pants, put his hand down my pants, and grazed his finger across my vagina. "Stop," I whispered in fear and shame, but he didn't respond or listen. He continued to touch me, moving my panties to the side, and putting his finger in my vagina. I grabbed his hand, trying to move it from my vagina. "Please stop," I whispered as I tried to get down from the countertop, but he just pushed me back on the countertop and put his finger back into my pants and into my vagina. He whispered back, "You know you like it. They liked it, too." Amongst so many other things, I thought, *Who the hell are they?* Then it came to me — he was talking about Lyfe and Fifi. I cried silently, tears streaming down my face waiting for it to be over. I was good at crying silently — it was something I learned at my mother's house. The countertop was on my right of the kitchen door entrance, so he kept looking to his right to peek out of the kitchen while he kept one finger in my vagina and the other hand around my back checking to see if Grandma was still outside. The only thing I could think of was that night in my bedroom, trying to look at his body to see if it was his silhouette I saw in the dark. Uncle P whispered, "Did you like that the other night?"

"It was you!!" I muttered quietly, still silently crying.

He whispered, "Remember what I said," as he pushed into my vagina deeper before taking his finger out. He left me on the countertop as he walked out of the kitchen. I didn't even look up at him as I jumped down from the countertop, zipped up my pants, and went upstairs to my room feeling defeated, used, nasty, and scared. I never ate my bowl of cereal. I was hungry, but I just couldn't get over what had just happened. I cried in my room for a minute, then I got out of my clothes and into the shower before Grandma came back into the house. *I didn't want her yelling at me for taking a second shower already.* I thought back to the times when I was living with my mother, and my sister would make me do nasty things to the boys on the block so that they could pay her money. I felt so disgusted with myself and so small. I felt like I was nothing but a boy toy. I didn't understand why. *I'm not even pretty,* I thought. I was skinny as sticks and bones as everyone else would say and wasn't fully developed yet. But somehow, I was always used as a pleasure doll. The sexual abuse didn't stop there on the countertop. Uncle P continually found ways to get me alone and touch me inappropriately. He also continued to sneak into my room to rape me a few times a month.

The next few times he came into my room to rape me, I squirmed and moved to try to stop him from succeeding, but he was too strong. He used the same restraints as before, and the same message to silence me. As he continued to sneak into the house and into my room, eventually I stopped squirming and moving and let him handle his business. In my mind, I had no hope. *I can't beat him because he is stronger, I can't tell on him because no one will believe me over him, and maybe if I don't move it will be over soon,* was my thought process. Flashbacks of how Lyfe pimped me out

117

ran through my head while I was being raped, which also crippled my body into submission with Uncle P. I just laid there silently with tears running down my cheeks and to the back of my ears depending on the position we were in — a skill I learned from my mother because I wasn't allowed to make noise when I cried in pain. I just had to take it and move on with this secret because other than this struggle, life was good here, and for some odd reason, I still felt like family.

It was so hard keeping this secret from everyone, but I honestly didn't want to make anyone upset with me. Other than being raped by Uncle P, I pretty much enjoyed the family I was living with, so I found a way to ease the blow of being raped. As I made friends I would ask to stay the night over at their houses, and most of the time the answer was yes. Grandma took a while to come around to the idea of me staying the night over at people's houses. In the beginning, her answer would be no. She would say, "Why do you wanna sleep in someone else's bed when you have your own bed?" but as I got a little older and busier with sports and activities, she let me stay over at my friends' houses. My friends didn't know that they were saving my life and giving me relief from the pain of being sexually abused. Being around them made it easier for me not to recognize that I was taken from one pot of hot water and placed into another pot of boiling hot water. I was so damaged by my mother that I was willing to endure this new struggle dressed in nice clothes, nice styles, and my own bedroom. As a problem solver, this was one way I thought I was solving the problem, by staying away as much as possible. Of course, I didn't stay the night every night over at someone's house; so, Uncle P still made it to my room some nights, but not as much as before. On the nights I was away, I wondered, *did he come for me today? I hope he gives up and just stops coming forever. I hope he gets caught by Grandmom.* Although it gave me relief to stay at my friends' houses, the relief was only temporary before I started being touched and raped by the brothers of my friends.

CHAPTER NINE
MR. TERRANCE

I was 17 years old, and it was the last summer I would be able to participate in the drill team because I was aging out and leaving for college soon. I was part of The Haddington Sophisticated Ravens Drill Team, led by Mr. Scoot, the director. The supervisor was Mr. Terrance, and Mr. Scoot's daughter, Jazmine, was the captain. After a month of stepping and proving myself, I became the co-captain alongside Jazmine. The drill team was fun. We had practice twice a week and competitions a few times a month. It was a way for me to get away from home- *really to get away from Uncle P, who was still visiting my room a few times a month without my grandma knowing.* There were teenage girls and boys on this drill team, which normally made it easy to hook up with each other, but Mr. Scoot was overprotective about the team and would shut down any sign of matchmaking. He was like the father of the team; he didn't play, and neither did we for the most part. I felt safe when I went to drill team practice. I felt comfortable and free around Mr.

Scoot. I felt so safe with him that I started working under the table as a paper girl. *Yup, I was a paper girl making $9 an hour tax-free; the hustle was real.* Mr. Scoot asked me if I would work for him throwing papers to houses at 5 a.m., and I said yes excitedly. Surprisingly, my grandma let me do it, but I think she respected my drive to work, and Jazmine was working as well. I got to know Jazmine and Mr. Scoot better, but perhaps I felt too free at practices because Mr. Terrance was watching my every move *literally,* and suddenly, I felt like prey. It didn't matter how far apart we were in a room; he was watching me like a hawk, waiting for me to be isolated by the team so he could scoop me up and take me away. Whenever he had the chance, he would hover over me, digging his talons into my shoulder, standing face to face, or moving me out of the way with his hands on my waist. I wasn't as safe, comfortable, or free as I thought. I felt like I was being hunted.

Mr. Scoot was a widower in his late 50s, caring for his daughter Jazmine and about 10 other girls and boys who were on the drill team. He was very fatherly, not only to Jazmine but also to the rest of the team, though mostly to Jazmine. Jazmine was a year older than me and a little taller than me, with light skin and hair down to her shoulders. Her teeth weren't perfectly straight, but she was skinny with a curvy body and was very flirtatious. After all, growing up, most boys liked light-skinned girls, and she loved herself in her skin. She would come to drill practice with a sweat suit on and then take it off when she got hot, revealing a belly tank top that showed off her flat stomach and C-cup breasts. Mr. Terrance would tell her to put her sweatshirt back on, and Jazmine would get mad. Jazmine had a temper, or perhaps she was just spoiled because she would argue with Mr. Scoot.

"Oh, my God, Dad! I'm not a little girl anymore, and it's hot! Why do I gotta put this sweatshirt back on?" Jazmine protested.

"You don't need to be showing off your body. There are boys and men around. Put your sweatshirt back on," Mr. Scoot calmly replied.

"Oh, I hate you!" Jazmine yelled as she grabbed her sweatshirt and put it over her head.

"Don't talk to your father like that, young lady," he softly scolded.

Mr. Scoot never yelled at his daughter or the team. I couldn't believe Jazmine was talking to her father like that in front of the entire team. In the Black community back in the day, it was not common for children to talk back to their parents because they would get backhand smacked so fast and hard, they would forget where they were. Mr. Scoot didn't hit his daughter; he punished her for weeks and took things from her that she loved or cherished. He treated Jazmine the same way he treated us; he just repeated himself until we did what he told us to do. Jazmine wasn't allowed to have body parts out and neither were we during practice. "To all the ladies, you will come to rehearsal fully clothed. I don't want to see any bellies or bottom parts because it's not appropriate," Mr. Scoot announced to everyone at almost every practice. If anyone showed up to practice dressed inappropriately, he would make them go home and change. I loved that about Mr. Scoot. He was a protector and not an abuser of his authority. Mr. Scoot was at most of the rehearsals, but because he had other jobs, he would sometimes leave rehearsal early and leave Mr. Terrance in charge of the team, which changed everything.

Mr. Terrance was a nice "Christian" man who encouraged and prayed for the team before every competition. He always wore a four-piece suit to practice and competitions, which made him look older than his actual age. Despite being younger than Mr. Scoot, he somehow looked older in a way. Mr. Terrance was 37 years old and about 5'4", which was the same height as me. He was skinny with dark skin, big, popping eyes, and horrible teeth. There were missing teeth all over his mouth, and the few teeth he had left were stained with plaque, tartar, and whatever else made his teeth look like gold. His breath smelled bad, the worst I had ever smelled before. It was a running joke within the drill team that Mr. Terrance would melt your face off when he talked to you if you were too close during a conversation. It was really that bad; it was halitosis at its worst. Despite this, he was still a nice person, just with really, bad breath. He was helpful to everyone and always smiling. Although a little tougher than Mr. Scoot, he was kind and kept us focused and well-behaved during rehearsals. However, Mr. Terrance became a little too friendly and kind to me in a subtle way. He started to call my house to remind me of rehearsals and competitions in the afternoons before they began. At practice, he told me that I was doing a great job learning the steps and dances and finding ways to complement my every move.

"You must have been on a drill team or dance team before. You are doing really well!" Mr. Terrance complimented.

"Thank you! I've only danced in the dance ministry at church. This is my first drill team!" I explained excitedly.

It felt good to be complimented on my work. After all, I was trying something new to stay busy and out of trouble. I have to admit, I was a great stepper and dancer. I stepped with pride and danced with purpose. North Philly taught me how to dance. I had snuck out of the house a few times when my mother was gone and won so many dance battles at the park. So, I knew what I was doing and how to move. Living with my mother, I wasn't allowed to join any extracurricular activities at school, let alone in the community, so I had to sneak out. This was big for me. I didn't have to sneak around, and I was part of a community when I was on the drill team. Obviously, it looked good on me. If no one else noticed me, Mr.

Terrance sure did, and it felt good to be noticed in a positive way, at least I thought it was a positive way.

As time passed, Mr. Terrance began showing me more kindness. He would call my house later in the evening after drill practice to tell me how well I was doing and how happy he was that I joined the team. During practice, he would stare at me while I danced. At first, I thought it was normal because he had to look at everyone, but the way he looked at me made me feel uneasy. While he would look at all the girls, his gaze lingered on me as if he were lost in a daydream. I couldn't tell if he admired my skills or me as a person. He would offer me water after I had been dancing for a while, and I would accept it. Dancing and stepping required a lot of energy, and it's easy to become dehydrated, so I took his offer. On one occasion, he noticed a button on the back of my shirt was unfastened, so instead of telling me to fix it myself, he decided to do it for me. While I was talking to Jazmine, Mr. Terrance walked behind me and touched the back of my neck to reach the unfastened button. It caught me off guard, and I stepped away, grabbing the back of my neck and turning around to see what was happening. At first, I thought it might have been a bug, and I was about to freak out. Mr. Terrance laughed and explained that he was just fastening my button because it was loose. He offered to do it for me because I couldn't reach it. He walked behind me and got as close as he could to fasten the button, and his breath blew on me, singeing the hairs on the back of my neck as the smell of his breath was overwhelming. I cleared my throat and held my breath until he finished fastening the button. Afterward, he flashed me his golden smile and called me "beautiful." It made me sick to my stomach on so many levels, especially the smell of his breath. There were other instances where he would wipe a piece of lint off my shoulder or move me out of the way of a buzzing bee or other insects, just so he could touch me. One day, while waiting for a parade to start, he stepped behind me, grabbed me by my waist, and pushed me aside so "I wouldn't get stung by a bee." Of course, I didn't see the bee and was grateful that I didn't, because I probably would have freaked out. It wasn't until later that I noticed the pattern of him getting into my personal space to somehow touch me. Then I started to receive late-night phone calls from him after practice.

One night after practice, he called my house, and instead of talking about the drill team, we talked about other things, things I didn't expect to hear.

"Hi Tameena, look, I have something to tell you, but I don't want you to get creeped out!" Mr. Terrance warned me.

"Hi, Mr. Terrance, what's up? Why would I be creeped out?" I asked.

"It's just that I like you; I feel like we have a connection at drill team practice, and I want to get to know you better," he said.

There was a pause of silence because I didn't know what to say. I mean, I knew what I should have said, but it just took me some time to take in what just happened.

I whispered, "But you're way older than me. We can't be together or anything like that." I didn't want my grandma to hear this conversation.

"Listen, I know it sounds crazy, but I believe God had us meet and gave me this feeling for a reason. You believe in God, don't you?" Mr. Terrance said smoothly.

"I believe in God, Mr. Terrance, but I am only 17. You are like 30-something, and I can't date anyone that old," I said in a matter-of-fact way.

"I'm 37, and age ain't nothing but a number. People do it all the time, getting with people older and younger than them. You just have to know what you want and go for it, Tameena. I see the way you look at me during practice, and you like the way I treat you. Give it a try. We can start off really slow. I just want to get to know you better," he explained.

I knew this old man was up to something, but he said it in such a convincing tone. At that moment, he made me feel like I was old enough to make my own decisions about who I date, and who gets access to my body. He made it sound right. *Boy, I was so naive-don't judge me, y'all, love me.* For the first time, I felt like I had the power to choose what I did with men; instead of being taken advantage of, and being molested and raped by older men, I could make the decision of who I would allow access to me. In that instance, I felt a sense of empowerment over my body and over my circumstances.

Mr. Terrance was not attractive to me in any way, but I wanted to experiment, and without too much thought, I responded, "Okay, let's try it, but if it doesn't work, it doesn't work!" *I finally have control over myself and what I want to do,* I thought.

"Okay, if it doesn't work, it doesn't work Tameena!" Mr. Terrance said with a chuckle.

"I will see you at practice, and by the way, no one has to know about this; it won't look right, so let's just keep this between us," I whispered before saying goodnight.

"It's our little secret," he responded before we hung up the phone.

The next practice Mr. Terrance stole a few looks at me while I danced, but I literally paid him no mind. I was showing him that I did not want to make it known. I didn't even want anyone to get an inkling that something was going on. He wasn't extra; meaning overtly obvious, but he just continued to find ways to get in my personal space and touch me somehow; thankfully it was not noticeable enough to bring anyone's attention to us. At the end of practice that night, I was riding the bus going home, when I put my hands in my pocket and found $50. *What the, where did this come from?* I said to myself. I was confused for a second, but then I thought about Mr. Terrance. *He must have put this in my pocket. I guess he's gonna be my sugar daddy now. Yeah, I'm gonna play this; I don't even get to give up no ass for this,* I thought to myself on the bus. When I reached home, Mr. Terrance called my house to make sure I got home and that I had got the money.

"Hello Tameena, you looked great tonight! Did you get the little something I left in your pocket?" he asked with pride.

"Hi Mr. Terrance, I did, and thank you so much!" I responded.

"You don't have to call me Mr., You can just call me Terrance when we talk outside of the drill team!"

"Ok, Terrance, thank you very much. I have to go now; my grandma is coming." I said in a rush.

"Ok, I will see you at practice. Bye, Tameena," he whispered.

"Bye Terrance," I said as I rushed off the phone.

Our relationship was the same for about the next few weeks. He would sneak different things into my pockets like bracelets, money, and movie tickets for me to find on my way home. I met Mr. Terrance at the movie theater on 69th Street a few times on our off days from drill team practice. I lied to Grandma that I was going out with some of my girlfriends, but I was really going out alone with Mr. Terrance. When Terrance first saw me at the movie theater, he walked up to me, putting his arms around me as he attempted to kiss me. I moved his arms from around me and backed away from his face before his breath could reach my nostrils.

"We are in public. We have to look like father and daughter, not like boyfriend and girlfriend," I said frantically, trying to keep the facade and also dodge his breath.

"Oh yes, you are right. Well, fathers and daughters hold hands. Can we hold hands?" Terrance asked, unsure of the answer.

"I guess, hopefully, no one we know sees us, so they don't suspect anything. I really can't get caught with you, Terrance!" I mentioned it in panic.

He grabbed my hand and said, "Relax, as soon we see anyone we know, we can separate. I'm glad to even be here with you right now. We can stay secret as long as we need."

We enjoyed our movie sitting next to each other and holding hands. At the end of the movie, he stole a kiss from me while we were still sitting in the chairs during the credits. He kissed me right on the cheek, *and I almost threw up in my mouth.* I couldn't believe he had just done that with his stinky breath.

I turned to him and whispered, "Terrance, listen, to be honest, your breath smells really bad, and if we are going to kiss, you have to fix your breath!"

"I was waiting for you to say something. I have halitosis, which is why my breath smells. Sometimes I can handle it, but sometimes I can't, so be patient with me while I work on it. I will make sure I do all I can before kissing you," he whispered with an embarrassed look on his face. *You should be embarrassed, you're a grown-ass man with your breath smelling like shit,* I thought to myself, hoping my thoughts didn't leave my mouth.

"Okay, thank you for letting me know. I just thought you didn't brush your teeth or anything," I said, relieved that he does. We left the theater and went our separate ways to go home. Terrance and I dated each other for 3 months after this, sneaking out together and giving kisses on the cheek to keep things slow, and for me not to catch halitosis in my mouth.

Terrance continued to call my house after each practice when Grandma started questioning what was going on between Terrance and me. One night after I got home from practice, he called and Grandma picked up the phone that was in her room.

"Hello, wh-wh-who is this? I knew it was him, but it was too late. I sneakily picked up the phone that was in my room, holding the bottom of the receiver up away from my mouth so she wouldn't hear me breathing to eavesdrop on her conversation. *Do y'all remember those clear phones, the ones that showed the wiring inside the phone? I had one of those phones in my room. I thought I was all that.* Well, I didn't need to eavesdrop; my Grandmom spoke loud enough for me to hear her in my room three rooms down, but I needed to hear Terrance's responses.

"Why do you ke-ke-keep calling for Tameena this ti-ti-time of night?" Grandma asked with an attitude.

"Um, I was just making sure she got home safe after practice, ma'am," Terrance lied through his missing teeth.

"She is fine. Please st-st-stop calling her this late, or I am going to c-c-call the cops on you for stalking a minor!" Grandma promised. There was a pause after that statement, and then she hung up the phone and marched her way to my room. I hurried and hung up the receiver before she got into my room yelling, "Tell that man to st-st-stop calling here for you! You don't think I know you have been s-s-sneaking out with him, and talking on the ph-ph-phone with him?" I was caught off guard; I didn't think she knew any of that, and maybe she was fishing the truth out of me to get me to admit it.

"Grandmom, he only calls to make sure I got home safe from practice. He does that to all the girls on the team!" I lay in a shaky voice, trying not to give myself away.

"Tameena, no man is going to c-c-call you this much this time of night just to make sure you got home unless he likes you, you've been g-g-going out with him. I know you're lying, and I won't have you b-b-being fast in my house. I won't!" Grandma fussed, pointing at me.

"I am not going out with him, and I am not fast!" I yelled. I had never talked back to my grandma, let alone yelled at her. She knew I was lying.

"If he k-k-keeps calling here, I'm t-t-taking you off the drill team; I mean it Tameena! I dealt with enough w-w-with your sisters, I am not going through this with you!" she yelled, yanking my phone out of the socket. "Since you want to b-b-be fresh, you won't have a ph-ph-phone, and don't a-a-ask for it back because I-I-I won't give it back!" she continued as she stormed out of my room.

I was going through an internal battle with myself. I was embarrassed, and I felt bad for lying to my grandma because she took good care of me, but I also wanted to yell, *you don't really care; your son is raping me for God's sake. You couldn't figure that out, but you just know this little deal.* My feelings were hurt because she called me fast, although, I have been called much worse by my own mother. I've been called a "hussy," "bitch," "slut," and "whore" before I had ever done anything. So, when I heard my grandma call

137

me "fast" it took me aback and made me mangry (mad and angry) but I just kept it all in. At the next practice, I told Mr. Terrance that I could not talk to him anymore, and he agreed that it wasn't the right time. He stopped calling the house, we stopped going out, but he didn't stop making passes at me whenever he could sneak one in at practice. My Grandma dropped the issue, and she never called me fast again.

CHAPTER TEN
CHURCH

In the beginning, going to church was a nuisance because Grandma and I would go every Sunday from sun up to sun down. Maybe it wouldn't have been so bad if it weren't two or three services each Sunday. *Now don't get me wrong, I love Jesus, but I didn't know it required so many services to get a relationship with him (it doesn't).* There was a morning, afternoon, and sometimes evening service at another church, and Grandma made sure we went to every service. *Don't judge me, those services are long, like five hours each.* Not to mention there was Sunday School that took place before morning service started, which I had to attend. The good thing about going so much was that we ate between the second and third service. The church cook, Ms. Thelma, was amazing; she put her foot in everything she cooked. She would make fried fish, fried chicken, baked macaroni and cheese, yams, string beans, and desserts. *See, back in the day, you didn't have to pay for dinner between services; nowadays, everything costs money. You have to pay for the food, or sometimes the food is only for the people in leadership at the church; What's up with that?* Going to church every Sunday was a lot, and I didn't know what the hype was about God.

Part of my reluctance to attend church was because I didn't understand why people gathered every Sunday to go to church and praise a God who allowed me and so many other people in the world to go through hardships. When I first got saved (accepted the Lord Jesus Christ into my heart as my personal Savior), I was going through so much at home. My mother was abusing me on a daily basis, my sister Lyfe was pimping me out to boys, and my sister Fifi and I were always fighting each other. My emotions were all over the place. During that time, the chapel at camp was my safe haven. It felt good to be able to release all my emotions in a place where I would not be judged for crying. It gave me a temporary fix that made me feel like I could continue to live on, but I thought God was going to change my situation and make it better, but he didn't at that time. I went back home after camp, and the beatings continued, the pimping and fighting continued, and suddenly, I didn't see God as my personal savior anymore. I did not see him come to my house and save the day; he did not release my mother's hand from around my throat, nor did He stop Lyfe from hustling my body to the boys in the neighborhood. By the time I moved in with Grandma and joined her church, I was not enthused about going to church every Sunday to go through the new trauma of being a foster child, being abandoned, and living with the pain from my past. I would watch people sing, shout, dance, and pray to God, wondering how their individual lives were. *Were they doing all of this because they were living good lives? Are they not suffering the way I am suffering? Why are these people so happy living this life? Does God love them and not me?* were the thoughts that ran through my head as they performed. I had a heart of stone for a long time until I started making friends and joining different ministries in the church.

It seemed like everyone in the church was related to everyone like it was one big happy family. When I was first introduced to most of the people in the church, their names were prefixed as Sister or Brother so and so, but later these people became Aunt and Uncle, so and so. Everyone was so nice and kind to be around. Of course, you had a few people in the church who were bitter and negative, but for the most part, the whole church was very Kumbaya-ish, even to those visiting for the first time. As I continued to attend church every Sunday, I began to get closer to some of the other teenagers, and then began to join ministries to participate in at church. The church was filled with children, teens, and young adults so much that it looked like a K-12 school. Sunday school was fun in my class because the teacher was cool; her name was Sister Bella (Aunt Bella). There were about twelve to fifteen students in Aunt Bella's Sunday school class. We would have real-life discussions in Aunt Bella's class, and we would relate the Bible to what was happening in the real world. I loved going to her class to learn about God because it wasn't boring, and the way she taught made sense to me. Sometimes just listening to the pastor preach wasn't enough for the young people. See, we needed the word (Bible) to be broken down based on our level of understanding, *which was, at the time, anything that wasn't pointing fingers at young folks for not living right.* In Aunt Bella's Sunday school class, we could ask questions about the Bible, church, and God, and she would answer the best way she could and without judgment. At first, I felt shy in class and didn't want to speak up much, but then I opened up a little, still careful not to show my true identity, which was broken and abandoned. I didn't want to be the weirdo in the class; I wanted to get along with everyone and make friends. The whole class was good friends, but I especially got close to Jinniyah, who was Aunt Bella's daughter, and Tattiana, who was Jinniyah's cousin, and a few other teens from the church. Jinniyah and Tattiana made me feel like I was truly their friend, and we began to hang out, outside of church and were often together. If I'm totally honest, at this point in my life, attending church was more about gaining relationships with friends for me than gaining a relationship with God. *Don't judge me, love me; I'm just being transparent.* I was still apprehensively learning about this God who would allow bad things to happen to me, so I just focused more on developing human relationships with the people I met in the church.

There was this one human relationship that I gained in the church; it was with a boy whose name was Alejandro. *I had a little church boyfriend, which was hard to do because everyone in the church was like family, even newcomers.* One Sunday morning, this family of four walked into the church visiting for the first time. It was a mother, two sons and a daughter. The daughter was the oldest, a little older than me at the time, Alejandro was the middle child with a younger brother. Alejandero was 17; he was tall, and light-skinned, with short curly hair and had a nice smile. Tattiana and I spotted him at the same time and looked at each other in amazement of how cute he was, and we nudged Jinniyah to look at him.

"Gurl, look at him; he's so cute," I said.

"Yeah gurl, he is cute," Tattiana responded.

"He's alright," Jinniyah said, looking him up and down.

"I would go out with him," Tattiana added.

Throughout the rest of the service, we were talking about how cute he looked. Alejandro sat on the right side of the church, and he looked our way on the left side a few times during service.

I joined almost every ministry Jinniyah and Tattiana joined, and this helped me begin to love going to church more. *Oh, and my little church boyfriend helped me too*! I was excited to go to church to meet up with my friends and participate. The first ministry I joined was the children's choir, and although I knew how to sing and wanted to join, I only joined because Jinniyah and Tattiana were in the choir. I loved to sing, but I was conditioned not to when I was living with my mother, so I didn't even think about joining the choir before Jinniyah and Tattitana. It was a time that we could hang with them, laughing and clowning around. I sang in the children's choir well into my teenage years and up until I was able to sing in the young adult choir. See, in my church, we had a children's choir, a young adult choir, and the gospel chorus, *which was the senior citizen's choir.* Jinniyah and Tattiana had already stopped singing in the children's choir, and I was the tallest kid singing with all the little kids. After a while, they would say, "Girl, you like 20 still singing in the children's choir," and we would laugh, but I loved to sing, and my grandma wouldn't let me quit. So, I sang until I was able to join the young adult choir, *which was bumping (really good).* We sounded so good, and the songs were great songs that made everyone in the congregation hype by clapping, singing along, dancing, and, of course, praising God. When I was able to, I joined the young adult praise team that sang at 8 a.m. services, and we were okay, getting better and better as we continued to sing together. The older I got, the more I was able to sing on the adult praise team. Singing was one of the ways I could connect with God because I was able to feel his presence as the words of the song that I was singing to others spoke to me personally, but dancing was my favorite way to communicate with God.

Dancing was always part of my life, starting when I was living with my mother, but dancing in church was a lot different from dancing in the streets. The music was different, the dance moves were different, and the crowd was different. I remember the times when Lyfe would sneak me to the park to battle some girls in a dance battle for some cash. I was good at dancing; I would break out with the butterfly, the tootsie rolls, and the crybaby. Even though the crybaby required me to get on the ground, it was my favorite dance move because I would fall flat on the ground with my face on my right arm and my left arm out over my head, with my legs straight out, lifting my butt up and down, and lifting my left arm pounding it to the ground every time my waist hit the ground. The crowd used to go crazy when I did that move, and that was my finishing winning move on everyone I ever won against. I loved the expressions on my face while dancing; I loved the praise from the crowd; I just simply loved dancing. When I got to church and saw the type of dancing they were doing, I was shocked. To me, it looked like slow dancing, but later I learned it was a form of ballet, and some moves were mixed with some jazz and hip-hop. I didn't know I was going to get into it the way I did. I began to love praise dancing at church.

Praise dance was a way that I was able to communicate with God through my body. Since I loved music so much, I was able to feel the rhythm and beats of Christian songs and move to them accordingly. Jinniyah, Tattiana, and I joined the dance ministry at church along with about twelve others of my church friends. My dance choreographer Damion was a teenage boy who was and is a close friend of mine that attended church as well, and he was a great dancer, and still is to this day. The way Damion would move his body made me jealous at times; I wanted to be great like him, and he didn't play. It was like he was a real dance teacher (*which he is now; and owns a dance school).* He would do a loud clap or count

147

so we could keep the beat. If you weren't doing the moves right and with emotion, he would call you out and make you do it over until he liked the way it looked. Damion made us exercise and stretch, and before dancing, we even prayed and read the Bible to help us tap into the message of God we were going to be relaying through dance to the people in the congregation. For the most part, I was good at dancing once I learned the moves, but my one challenge was not being able to stop spinning. If there was a double spin and land with a plie, I would do like a triple or spin and land with a plie. I didn't know how to control my body to stop spinning in time for the next move. Nonetheless, dancing became my spiritual connection to God.

I would listen to the music over and over to let the music set in my spirit and apply the lyrics to my daily struggles, needs, and most of all my gratefulness to God for even being alive. One of my favorite dances was to the song "Blessed and Highly Favored" by The Clark Sisters, and if y'all know about the Clark Sisters, then you know this song is amazing. The song talks about how God has brought us through trials and tribulations and that we should realize that we are blessed and highly favored because we are still alive. Toward the end of the song, it repeats "It could've been me; it should've been me, it would've been me if it wasn't for the blood" about six times explaining that everything the devil tried to throw at us, God blocked it for our good. As we were listening to the song at rehearsal and trying to find dance moves, I think Jinniyah came up with the idea that we should all come up with a struggle that we ourselves struggled with, or a current struggle, or a struggle that we know someone else close to us may be dealing with that affects us. We each chose a struggle and went to choreograph our struggle into dance moves on our own, and kind of turned it into a game to see if we could guess each other's struggle. Each of us had about 20-30 minutes in our own areas in the church to create our dance parts. I won't go through all the struggles because that could be a chapter in itself and because I don't remember them all, but see if you could name our struggles based on how you are reading them.

Tattiana started by raising her left hand like it was holding something in the air. Then, whatever she was holding, she put to her mouth nodding her head all the way back and then forward, wiping her mouth with her right hand, staggering around, and then froze for the spotlight to be on Damion. Damion put both hands together pulling them apart as if he was stretching something. He wrapped whatever he was stretching around his arm just above his elbow and pulled it tight tapping his inner arm with two fingers. Damion held up his left hand making the letter L with his index finger and thumb and started plucking his index finger with his right hand. After he plucked his fingers, he poked his inner arm with the index finger he was plucking. As soon as he poked himself, Damion let out a sigh of relief smiling and leaning his head to the side, opening his eyes wide before he froze for Jinniyah to share her struggle. Jinniyah put both of her arms out in front of her looking at her wrists. She took her right hand, swiped across her left wrist, and then took her left hand and swiped it across her right wrist. She watched both wrists and took her right hand and then she put her right hand to her neck swiping it from left to right then hanging her head down with her eyes closed before she froze for the next struggle to begin. *I'm gonna give you a minute to process these struggles because I need a minute to process them while I'm writing this before I give you the last one.*

The last struggle is my favorite, *not because I like struggles, but because of the way it was acted out*. This struggle was played by Sister Star who was the oldest person in the dance ministry and new to dancing. Sister Star stretched both arms out to the side bringing them in toward her body while twiddling her fingers on both hands. She gathered her arms together, bringing her hands to her mouth and deeply inhaling and blowing into her hands. We had no idea what she was trying to act out — it was like a bad game of Charades. As teenagers, we looked at each other, and then turned away to hold our laughs in because we wanted to respect her struggle. *You know when you can hold in your laugh, but when you see someone else struggling to hold their laughs in and it makes you burst out into laughter — that's how we were trying to hold it together.* Everyone was watching Ms. Star closely, asking her to do it again so we could guess the struggle and the only answers we could come up with were witchcraft or playing the flute. *I don't know but it was giving jazz hands and flute player to me, but I know y'all trying to figure out our struggles.* Our struggles were: alcoholism played by Tattiana, heroin played by Damion, suicide played by Jinniyah, and crack cocaine played by Sister Star. *I bet y'all are still trying to figure out Sister Star's moves lol.* We were going to help her out and change the moves once she told us about her struggle, but she explained it in such a way that made us believe she struggled with this, which led us to believe she knows what she is talking about. So, we let Ms. Star dance it the way she knew it. Unfortunately, I don't remember what my struggle was in the dance, but I know that all the above could have been me. All the struggles that were chosen were already a part of my family's history and my personal history as well. This is what made the dance so much more effective and reached the people who watched us minister. The struggles we chose not only gave the depiction of what young children go through behind the smiles they wear, but it also shows what we saw as young children that have affected us. It shows the resilience and tenacity of what some adults experienced as children and young adults but have overcome their struggles. When I danced, I danced with a purpose to let the people in the congregation feel my movements hoping they would be moved by God. The entertainment ministries were awesome and are what led me closer to God, but it wasn't enough so I joined the GANG!

Like any gang, you must get initiated before you can join. The gang I joined, someone only needed to be 13 years old and attend church; *Some of you were probably thinking I joined a dangerous gang, Ha Got 'Em!* The GANG that I am referring to is my church youth group, **G**od's **A**nointed **N**ew **G**eneration, which was called GANG for short. The GANG would meet about twice a month, once in church and the other at Aunt Aza's apartment. Aunt Aza was the GANG leader, and she orchestrated all our outings and church activities. She was a minister in the church and was the kindest person I have ever met, like an angel in human form. Aunt Aza taught us the importance of living a godly life, and she encouraged us to do the right things and to follow Christ. I learned so much from the GANG meetings and the outings and had so much fun doing it, but it still wasn't enough to stop me from drinking and smoking. I was listening to the pastor preach, and I was reading the Bible, but I was still being molested and raped by Uncle P. I was still an orphaned child with no real family to call my own. It seemed nothing soothed the longing I had to become whole but smoking and drinking. The GANG would go bowling, skating, and on youth retreats. I would have had a great time, but when the fun was over and everyone went back to their homes, I had to go back to my reality of sexual abuse. Sometimes I would smoke and drink before I got to church; I would still sing in the choir, praise team, dance, and meet for GANG meetings while high or drunk, and no one knew, *at least I don't think anyone knew.* Most of the time, it didn't even bother me to be at church high or drunk, but there was this one time after school when I went to my friend's house and got high, but then went to choir practice at church afterward. I had on a sweater and long braids in my hair. I was sitting in choir rehearsal next to one of the mothers of the church, and I felt so bad because I thought she could smell the weed on me. *Y'all know that weed smell stays in your clothes and hair if you don't change your clothes right away.* I kept smelling my clothes and shrinking in my seat, thinking that everyone could smell me. No one said anything to me about the smell, but I was paranoid. Honestly, it was then that I thought I needed to stop smoking and drinking and try to let Jesus help me because, obviously, I can't help myself without digging myself into a deeper hole.

Whelp, if you can't beat them, join them, I thought one day when I decided to stop smoking and drinking and join the church people in trying to live holy lives. *Now, don't get me wrong, some of my fellow GANG members partook in some of my smoking and drinking habits as well.* Unlike me, they were raised in the church and had a great foundation in Jesus Christ that I was still learning. *No shade to my GANG members, because wrong is wrong and sin is sin once you learn that it's wrong.* It was time for me to quit the shenanigans and study the Bible so I could get to know the Jesus my pastor would preach about. I started reading the Bible on my own, not just when I was in church, and allowed it to minister to my spirit. When I had questions, I would ask them during GANG meetings, Bible study, and Sunday school. Eventually, I began to see my relationship change with God, other people, and myself. It was like I was going to church expecting to hear a word from God that I knew was going to help me live a better life despite what I was going through at home. At church, I learned that "All things work together for good

to them that love God, to them who are called to his purpose."
Romans 8:28. That was the scripture that kept me going because I
knew that even though I was going through so much, everything was
going to work out for me because I love God and I knew he had a
purpose for my life. I just had to stick it out. God became my outlet
to let out my fears and frustrations and to get rejuvenated. Church
was a place where I could cry out to the Lord, and it was normal
because almost everyone cried in church when they felt the Holy
Spirit, or when they needed the Holy Spirit, especially on youth
Sundays when Aunt Aza preached. Every time Aunt Aza preached,
it was like she was preaching from my diary. Some of the youth who
didn't go to church every Sunday came on fifth Sundays to hear
Aunt Aza preach. She acknowledged the struggles that we face and
told us how God sees what we are going through, but she gave
solutions on how to get over those struggles by giving them to God.
Going to church became another outlet for me to escape my heavy
sense of being alone and unwanted. For me, the church became like
the theme song to the TV show "Cheers." "Sometimes you wanna
go where everybody knows your name, and they're always glad you

came, you wanna be where you can see, the troubles are all the same, you wanna be where everyone knows your name." It was where I wanted to be because everyone knew me. This made me start to love attending church a lot more. I realized I needed church because God became what I needed to survive.

CHAPTER ELEVEN
HIGH SCHOOL YEARS

I attended West Philadelphia High School (SPEED BOYZ!)! High school was one of the highlights of my life! It was so much fun, mainly because Yani and I went to the same school and wherever you saw Yani, you caught me because we were always together. Yani and I joined sports and clubs, which made us proud Speed Girlz. West Philadelphia High School was "The One and Only" high school I attended, and they were the best school years of my life. *As you can see, I take pride in not jumping from high school to high school like I did in elementary and middle school due to fighting.* Yani and I were super excited to go to high school and make new friends, although we knew no one could stop us from being besties. *Shout out to my Bestie!!* I was especially excited because I was ready for a new scene kids. I was ready to get good grades, and ready to join varsity sports, but despite this, there were still things going on in my personal life that kept me from doing my best.

Yani and I hung out together most, and as planned, we made lots of friends throughout the four years from our freshman year all through our senior year. We were so excited about going to high school. "We're gonna join every group so we can be popular," Yani said as we were planning for high school. I would just be co-signing by saying, "Yup, we're gonna meet a lot of new people," as my brain reminded me of my introverted self, but I needed to join as many groups as I could because I thought it would keep my mind off being molested and raped by Uncle P and others; *yes, there were others, y'all*. So, I wasn't just co-signing; I was hoping to do fun things and meet new friends like the average teenager. I was hoping I would be able to go to high school and not be as angry and on edge as I was in middle school, but there is always someone to try me at the wrong time. There was this tomboy, named Qualita, who used to pick fights with people, to show off in front of the boys she hung around. Sometimes the boys paid her to fight certain people. One day, Qualita was standing in the doorway of the classroom with her foot sticking out to trip every person that walked into the classroom. Everyone else thought it was so funny, of course, except me. When it was my turn to walk into the classroom, Qualita stuck her foot out and said, "Go through."

I looked at her and said, "Move your feet," looking her up and down.

"Just go through!!" she yelled, yanking her head to the side.

I stood at the doorway with my arms crossed, holding my hands at my stomach, in my *keep playing with me* stance and said, "Qualita, don't touch me; I'm not playing with you."

The boys she was hanging with were hyping her up. One boy, Dookie, said "Ooooooh, she said don't touch her!" *Yani and I named him Dookie because he was dark with bad skin. The name stuck until we became adults. Back in the day, the stigma of having dark skin meant you were ugly, and if you had light skin, you were pretty. That was also, before I had my own mind; I love people no matter what color your skin you wear, now back to my story.*

"I bet you won't touch her," another one of the boys said.

Qualita saw that I wasn't playing with her and said, "You always so serious. I was only playing with you," and she moved her feet as I walked past to enter the classroom.

Dookie chimed in saying, "Ooooh, you gonna let her chump you like that, Lita," trying to hype Qualita up.

Qualita answered, "Nah, her sister and my sister are cool, so I'ma let her slide."

My sister Fifi and her sister Jaly fought a lot in school but then became friends, *which means Qualita knew about these hands,* but that was the closest I got to a fight in high school. People used to bother me because they liked to see me get upset, and before I got too mad, they would say, "Sike naw, chill." They knew when they went low, I went to hell! They didn't want no smoke (didn't want me to get really upset). Eventually, I started to get used to it and loosened up a little, and started to enjoy high school by keeping myself busy with extracurricular activities to get my mind off the struggles I was facing at home.

I joined a few sports teams like volleyball, basketball, and badminton. Volleyball was the most fun to play, though. My volleyball coach was a tall white man named Mr. Torch, who made me nervous during tryouts, because he looked so serious with no hair in the middle of his head. It turned out he wasn't serious. During tryouts he would tell jokes to let us know we were not doing that well like, "I passed you a ball and you didn't see it, here is another one," and he would toss another volleyball, but in a fun way to make us step up our game. I used his funny personality to forget about how badly I sucked last year in middle school and went on the court to do my thing, *hmmm who would've thought a man who didn't have hair in the middle of his head could be funny*. When I got on that court, I surprised myself; *somehow, I was good*. I was serving underhand and bumping the volleyball, *like hitting the ball*. I just had the basics, but at least I was good enough to make the varsity team! I was so surprised I made it and happy because I didn't want to do JV (Junior Varsity) with a team that played like I played in middle school. Even though I rode (sat on) the bench most of my freshman year because the seniors got more play time, it didn't matter; I was just happy to be part of the varsity team, and what made it more fun was that Yani made the team too; we rode the bench together. We were so excited because we got a chance to wear the uniform and a jacket with our names on it because we made it to the championships that year, and we felt like cool upperclassmen in our volleyball jackets. While riding the bench my freshman year, Coach Torch and his assistant, Coach Rose, really worked with me during practices to get me ready for next year. I got really good at practice and became part of the starting six lineup my sophomore year. Oh, I was goo; I could serve, spike, and dive for balls. In fact, I got so good that volleyball became my favorite sport to play.

Through everything I was going through at home, I found extracurricular activities and having fun with my different groups of friends at school as an outlet. West Philly High had a total of nine school periods, including a 0-period class, that started before school at 7:30 in the morning if you chose to participate. Some of the 0-period programs were chorus, band, and Reserve Officer Training Corps (ROTC). You had to be disciplined enough to get to school on time by 7:30 or you would be kicked out of the program. It didn't bother me to get up early, and it didn't matter how long I stayed up at night; my body was my alarm clock that woke me up at 5 a.m. I joined the school choir, which was totally amazing, *given that I liked to sing and stuff.* My choir director, Ms. Queen, was no joke. She did not play about time, and the time we spent in rehearsals were

164

productive. She was a musician outside of school, singing at different places on the weekends with her band. Ms. Queen had an operatic voice, very *doooooooooh, rrreeeeeeeee, meeeeeee, dooooooo; she held every note in a high-pitched range.* She wanted everyone to be in school by 7:15 so that we could start on time at 7:30, and I made sure I was on time (early) every morning, and so were the other choir members. I had so much fun during rehearsals and there was a major concert every year. Sometimes we sang at other high schools; it was such a great experience for me until I got caught up with the wrong crowd.

There were a few of the choir members I made friends with who were so cool to be around, but not necessarily good for me at the time. It was a way for me to escape from what I was going through at home. I hung out with four girls: Bev, Donna, Sandy, and Sasha. Sandy and Sasha were twins, who lived in a three-story house with about four or five bedrooms. Most of the time, we would all go to their house when their mother wasn't home to smoke and drink. Honestly, I never met their parents and was sure they lived alone as much as we were over there and how much we smoked. One day I was over at the twins' house with Bev and Donna, and we smoked

at least five joints in a circle, just passing them around. No one was

worried about any parents coming in and catching us and they didn't

worry about the smell of weed in the house. When I was living with

my mother and smoking, I smoked outside, so the smell wasn't in

the house when she got home. The twins didn't care; we didn't have

any windows open and some nights I was there all night, so I never

met their mother. The twins could sing very well, but Bev and

Donna had amazing voices. Bev had the better voice and could

serenade anyone to fall in love with her, girls, and boys. I, on the

other hand, could sing in harmony with other people, but not

necessarily as a soloist. For one, I was way too nervous to sing in

front of people for a solo, and two, I still wasn't used to singing

aloud in my house all willy-nilly. The lost voice I had while living

with my mother had damaged any chance, I had to be a comfortable

singer. I would just settle for singing in the background with my

found but disguised voice. My friends sound so good, that no matter

how much they smoked, it didn't stop them from being able to sing,

but for me, I wasn't so fortunate.

One night we had a concert at 6 p.m. I had taken my concert clothes to school so I could go to the twins' house after school to get dressed and then go back to the school from their house for the concert. After school, around 3 p.m., Bev, Donna, and I went to the twins' house, and we smoked a joint before getting dressed and leaving for the concert. We were all high, but chilling. I liked that group because they weren't wild and crazy after they smoked; they were chill like me. Yeah, we laughed and joked around, but for the most part, we were cool and not doing the most, just chillin'. We all walked to school together, hoping the smell of weed wouldn't be on us too bad, and it wasn't because we smoked before we got dressed. It was getting dark outside when we were walking to school for the concert when a dog started barking, ran out of the gate, and started charging toward us. Bev, Donna, and the twins started running in long skirts, but I froze. *I heard that when a dog is running toward you to stop because they don't attack you, that's what I did.* I stopped in the middle of the street, and the pitbull stopped right at my legs, barking, and jumping at me but not on me. Standing in fear, I heard my friends yelling out to me, "Meena, run," but I just stayed still until the dog's owner came outside and called to the dog. As soon as the dog went with its owner, I ran over to the girls, and we laughed and ran most of the way to school so we could make it on time for the concert. When we got to school and started our vocal warm-ups with Ms. Queen, I felt like I was whispering. I looked at the twins, signaling to them that I couldn't sing, as I pointed to my throat. The twins were smiling at me, wanting to laugh but not able to in front of Ms. Queen. When the twins, Bev and Donna started singing, they sounded better than how they sound when they were sober. I was struggling to get a tune out of my mouth, so I just lip-synced for the concert. Ms. Queen was looking at me, putting her hands to her ear, signaling that she couldn't hear me. Even though I was so embarrassed, I was cracking up inside because I was so high. After that concert, I told the twins that I cannot smoke before rehearsal or a concert, because that was crazy. No matter what was going on in my life, I made sure I was on time for choir rehearsals and concerts because I loved to sing and because I could hang out with my friends. Looking back, I can see that I had an addiction to numbing my pain with weed and alcohol and keeping myself busy with school activities, but I was functional and didn't let my addiction stop me from performing well in school.

Education was important to me in my fight not to become a statistic, but rather successful and independent. No matter how much I smoked and drank, I was determined to do well in school. I made sure I completed all my classwork and homework assignments for all my teachers, and I even studied a little bit for some tests. My business teacher, Ms. Truant, did not play; she was strict, but fun to be around. She taught me how to study, dress for school and business opportunities. When attending business trips, we couldn't board the bus to go anywhere without a full-dress suit. The gentlemen had to wear suits and ties, and the ladies had to wear pants or dress suits; but we had to have on suit jackets and stockings if we wore a dress, or we were not able to participate. She'd tell you to go home and get redressed, and hopefully, you would be able to make it back to the bus on time, because we were leaving on time with or without you. *I slay interviews because of how I dress and the preparation I learned from Ms. Truant. If you're reading this book, Ms. Truant: Thank you for preparing me for the real world and being the best teacher ever!* Ms. Truant enrolled Yani and me in this program, whose organization gave out monthly stipends for making good grades. The requirements were to just make A's and Bs with no more than one C to receive the $75 monthly stipend, *you know your girl came through with the clutch, aka survival mode, to get that money.* I didn't really get much of an allowance, so that $75 a month was a big deal for me, and it went a long way. It was used for lunch money, sometimes tokens or transpasses, and if I wanted to get myself a few things. There were times I pulled all-nighters to complete 5-10 paged papers, some of which may not have gotten done without the push of Aunt Sandi, *and when I say push, I mean a hard push. Aunt Sandi and I fought like cats and dogs when it was time for me to finish a paper or project.* I always waited until the last minute to start my work, because I was always a part of something and smoking and drinking, but I knew I had to pull through. My best work came after procrastinating because it put me in survival mode, a mode I was used to operating throughout my life, and that stipend was my incentive. Not only did my good grades get me money each month, but it gave me opportunities to be chosen to work good jobs while in high school.

Towards the end of 9th grade, Ms. Truant offered me and Yani a paid internship at State Representative James Roebuck Jr.'s Office. We were good at typing and good with Microsoft Office in class, *we were the two highest students in the class,* and the job required typing and filing. Yani and I made $9 an hour, *what fourteen-year-old you know was making $9 an hour in 1998?* and at that time, minimum wage was about $5.00 an hour. Although we worked a few hours a day, we felt like we were making a lot of money, which we were doing according to the minimum wage. In 10th grade, Ms. Truant offered me another paid internship working at Comcast Cable as an assistant to the secretary. The secretary, Ms. Sheena, used to be a student at West Philly High, and Ms. Truant was her teacher. Ms. Sheena needed help, so she asked Ms. Truant for a responsible and hardworking student who could type and file papers. *That's right, it was me. I was the weed-smoking, alcohol-drinking, responsible, and hardworking student who was chosen for the job.* I went on an interview and everything and slayed that

171

interview, thanks to the training I got from Ms. Truant. The dress code was business casual, so I had to wear dress clothes every day, which made me feel like a real businesswoman, *even though I was just typing and filing papers.* I started out making $9 an hour and moved up to $11 in my senior year. During my senior year, I was able to work more hours because I had a working roster, where I went to school for half the day and then worked the other half. The money I was making as a high schooler was good, so good that I started buying my own clothes, getting my own hair done, and saving money in the process. My work roster made it easier for me to be able to focus on schoolwork and the internship. Although I was busy, I still did my best in school to get good grades.

Senior year started in disaster with the traumatic experience of the terrorist attacks on 9/11, first in New York, and then in my home state. I remember having to evacuate school early because of the threat of another terrorist attack in Pennsylvania. It was one of the most devastating things I watched on TV, as the first and second planes crashed into the Twin Towers. Then, watching innocent people jump out of windows as the buildings collapsed to the ground like a flat pancake. Life already felt uncertain to me, but when 9/11 happened, it made me realize that one minute we could be here and the next we could be gone. *I would love to say that I got my act together and stopped smoking and drinking after my realization, but I didn't. It just made me more aware of my surroundings, and it taught me to live my life to the fullest- until it's gone.* While juggling the uncertainty of the real world, home life, school, and work, I was still able to graduate high school with A's & B's.

Graduation day came, and I was depressed because I didn't have any of my biological family there to celebrate me, but my Aunt Sandi was there to support me, and she made me feel better. I thought that family was only blood you know, the people I was born from and into, but I later learned that family isn't just those that have the same blood running through their veins. Family consisted of people who cared, supported, and encouraged you. *I learned that blood is not always thicker than water.* At graduation, I was awarded the Gift of Roses, which was given to the top two students in the Business Charter. Yani and I were the top two students in the Business Charter to receive the award. Receiving the award was such a surprise to me because I didn't even know The Gift of Roses was a thing. It was literally a bouquet of roses along with a certificate. The roses were beautiful, and it was the first time I had ever received flowers. Not only did I receive The Gift of Roses, but I also received a full scholarship to any college or university of my choosing from one of my favorite teachers, Mrs. Juliano. Mrs. Juliano was the athletic director who gave out one scholarship of the Arts to one student, and that one student was me. I was so surprised, and in that moment, I saw that God had better plans for my life. This meant I had to go to college because it was going to be free. Prior to graduation, Yani and I went to the counselor's office to pick out colleges to attend. I was not excited about it at all; I just knew I wouldn't be able to attend college because I didn't have any parents to pay for college, or anyone to take out any loans on my behalf, so I just counted it as a loss. If it wasn't for Yani, I wouldn't have applied to any colleges, but she encouraged me to, and I am glad I listened. Everything was working itself out for me in just enough time to give me hope for a brighter future. I got accepted into the three colleges I had applied to: Lincoln University, Indiana

University of Pennsylvania, and West Chester University. I chose to attend Lincoln University because that was where Yani was going. Although my graduation day started out rough, there were so many surprises and moments that encouraged me not to give up on myself. Graduation ended with the last song sung by the graduating class of '02, "We Haven't Finished Yet" by The 5 Heartbeats. The chorus says, "No matter how hard it gets, we haven't finished yet, there's so much of life ahead, we've got so much to do. No matter how hard we try, we just can't say goodbye, don't leave me with regrets 'cause we haven't finished yet!" As a lover of music, I left graduation feeling empowered and ready to enter the real world as a young adult.

CHAPTER TWELVE
COACH ROSE

Coach Rose was great as a volleyball coach, but she was also great as a mentor. She worked for a Christian-based community organization called Young Life which served young children, teens, and teen moms with resources and activities and provided them with different adventures and life-changing experiences. Coach Rose was a Young Life mentor and introduced Yani and me to the program. She became my mentor for a long period of time- *about a strong four solid years. She is still around if I need to talk.* She took me to meetings with the organization, where I met some amazing young people like me (foster children, and children who were abused). I considered our relationship to be as close. I've been to her house, and we went to outdoor gatherings. I visited her church a few times; Rose was a great Christian role model for me. We had Bible studies together, and the Christian advice she would give me was well-needed at the time. Our relationship began to deepen as time went by, and with the increased trauma I experienced, she was there to comfort me. I remember when she comforted me during the time when my 4-month-old niece passed away; this happened while I was living with Grandma. My sister Lyfe showed up at my door for the first time in about two years asking me to babysit my niece Alexis, whom I had never known or met before.

"Hey Meena, can you watch Alexis for me, and I will be back to get her later?" Lyfe asked.

"Hi Lyfe, How are you, and whose baby is this?" I responded and asked.

"This my daughter, and your niece, I have to do something, and I need you to watch her for me real quick," Lyfe hurried to pass me with my niece.

"Well, what is her name? I have to ask Grandma," I asked as Lyfe started walking away.

The next thing I knew, Lyfe left me at the door with a baby in my hand and a diaper bag at my feet. I called for Lyfe, but she never turned back. When I went back into the house and closed the door behind me, I called for Grandma.

"Grandmom, Grandmom!" I yelled.

"What is it, M-M-Meena!?" Grandma answered. She started to come down the stairs to the front door, and she was shocked to see me holding a baby. "Whose b-b-baby do you have?" Grandma asked.

"It's Lyfe's baby. She asked me to watch her for a little bit, and she would be back to pick her up later," I responded, scared for Grandma's response.

"Wh-Wh-," Grandma started before I interrupted.

"Grandmom, I tried to tell her I had to ask you first, but she just handed me the baby and ran off," I explained.

I was so excited to see Lyfe, to know that she was alive, and was excited to see my niece, by blood niece. I asked my grandma if I could watch her for the day, and she said yes, not realizing that Lyfe was trying to get rid of her baby for a few days. Alexis was so cute, so small- a little chocolate drop, but after about day three, I noticed that she cried a lot. I did everything I knew to calm her down — I fed her, changed her, held her, and took her to the porch for some fresh air. She would not stop crying; something in my spirit told me to just look at her as she cried. As I held her in my hands, with my arms stretched out in front of me, I watched her face. I noticed that her head wasn't really moving as she cried. I put my finger in front of her face to see if she would follow it and she didn't. Alexis was staring me dead in the face and she couldn't see my finger moving from left to right. I knew something was wrong because she wasn't following my finger. *Did she lose her sight*? I thought to myself. When she came to me, she could see, at least I thought she could. I didn't really know anything about her, so I just assumed she could see and then went blind while she was with me. Lyfe came to pick her up on the fourth day but didn't say thank you or anything; she gathered her things and just walked out of the house with Alexis. She looked like she was in a hurry or something; I was so angry with her for leaving her daughter with me for so long that I didn't even greet her, and neither did she greet me. Before she rushed off, I told her, "I think something is wrong with Alexis. She has been crying non-stop for the past two days," I explained.

"She is a baby; she always cries like that," Lyfe said.

"No, but this cry was different, Lyfe. I couldn't console her with anything," I explained further.

"That's because you don't know what you're doing!" Lyfe said with an attitude as if she thought I knew how to care for an infant.

"Well, why would you just leave her with me if you didn't think I could take care of her? You should've never bought her here. I am your younger sister. Just hurry up and leave with your dumb ass," I fussed.

Lyfe got the baby things together, picked up Alexis, and walked out of the door without saying goodbye. Two weeks later, Lyfe came back to Grandma's house to tell me that Alexis had died in her crib of SIDS (sudden infant death syndrome).

"She died," Lyfe said with no expression on her face.

"What do you mean she died? Who died?" I asked, not thinking about Alexis.

"Alexis, she died in her crib two days after she came back home from you; the funeral is this Saturday," Lyfe explained, still with no expression, handing me the death announcement card before walking away.

For a moment I was in shock, not knowing what to do or what to say. I was so hurt and wondered if it was something I didn't do right while she was with me. Babysitting Alexis was kind of therapeutic for me because I had someone to take care of someone who was part of my own family. I enjoyed it when I bathed, clothed, changed, sang to, and talked to Alexis. I looked forward to doing it again but that would never happen because she died. I partly blamed Lyfe because she was on drugs and her baby's father was as well; I thought maybe they neglected Alexis, and she died of neglect. My emotions were all over the place. I told Grandma about Alexis as well as Coach Rose. When the time came, Coach Rose took me to the funeral.

As Rose and I pulled up to the church where the funeral took place, silent tears escaped my eyes. I got out of the car and attempted to walk up the church stairs with Rose behind me. As I reached the top step and grabbed the door, my knees buckled, and Rose was there to hold me up and walk me through the church doors.

"It's gonna be OK, Tameena; you can do this if you want to, and if you don't want to, we can turn around," She Coach Rose encouraged.

"I can't do this; I want to, but I can't," I cried.

Rose continued to walk me into the church, and as I saw this little wooden box in front of the church, I began to weep. The box was about 30 inches long; and it was so small. It reminded me of when I held her in my arms. I walked up to the front of the church to see my niece, but the box was closed so that no one could see Alexis. Lyfe was on the left of the box with her baby's father and a few other people who were in the church. Lyfe was high, and so was her baby's father. I could see it in their eyes and in their body language, *and to be honest, I wished I was high at that moment too, so I didn't have to feel all the pain I was experiencing.* Lyfe was in charge of the program, and surprisingly, I was on it to sing a song. I had no idea that I was going to be asked to sing, and I didn't have anything planned. *First off, how did Lyfe know I could sing, or that I would sing?* I didn't feel like I had a choice, so I picked a song that had been my favorite at the time, "Hold On (Change is Coming') by

Sounds of Blackness. The lyrics to the song described how I tried to live my life through the hurt and trauma I'd endured: "Yesterday, a man step to me, He said, "How can you smile when your world is crumbling down?" I said, "Here's my secret, when I wanna cry, I take a look around and I see that I'm getting by, and I hold on, change is coming, hold on, don't worry bout a thing, hold on, you can make it, hold on, everything will be alright." I cried the entire time I sang the song, just as the tears are flowing from my face now as I write these lyrics to you. It was my favorite song until I sang it at Alexis's funeral; I hadn't sung the song since. Every time I hear the song, I would turn the station; I just can't go back to the pain I felt that day. Coach Rose was with me the entire time, supporting me, holding me up in prayer, and physically holding me up when my limbs gave out on me. Thank you, Coach Rose, for being there for me when I needed someone to keep me strong throughout my personal life in high school.

CHAPTER THIRTEEN
BREAKING SILENCE

High school was fun, but I went through some challenges at Grandma's house. School became my anchor; it kept me going. Freshman year was particularly challenging for me because I was still being sexually abused by Uncle P occasionally. This affected my self-esteem and hindered me from being my best self. This had been happening for the past four years, and I was exhausted from enduring that painful situation time and time again. One thing I noticed about myself was that I tend to suffer in silence to maintain peace. However, I also learned that prioritizing peace for everyone else only caused mental, emotional, and physical harm to myself. My first memory of being touched inappropriately was with my brother, who used to tickle me while he touched me around and, in my underwear, when I was about six or seven years old. I had no idea that my innocence was stolen at that age. As I matured, gaining an understanding of right and wrong, I felt as though I had commodified myself to life, allowing my body to be used inappropriately in exchange for peace. My body became a commodity for men, starting with my sister Lyfe, who exposed me to the boys on the block by threatening to tell my mother about something I did in the past, she even threatened to make up a lie. To avoid added confrontation with my mom, I did what Lyfe told me to do. Then, with Uncle P, to maintain my residence with Grandma. I experienced nightly abuse, and there were many other encounters whose stories will remain untold. This wasn't working for me. I knew I had to do something. Something had to change.

During my junior year of high school, I believed it was time to break my silence about what was happening to me at Grandma's house with my social worker. I didn't know what the outcome would be — whether I would still be able to live with Grandma, if I would have to move again, or if he would face consequences for what he was doing to me. My mind wouldn't get past questioning if Grandma was going to believe me. All these years, I wondered how I would be treated from here on out, and a flood of thoughts bombarded my head, making it hard for me to speak up. At this point in my life, I was fed up and feeling an urgent need for something more — something that didn't involve being molested and raped, so I finally mustered the strength to unleash my painful secret.

One day, during a visit with my social worker, Mrs. Bartanue (Ms. B), I made the decision to reveal my secret. I wasn't sure how, but I knew I had to find a way. Ms. B was among my favorite social workers because she checked in with me monthly, as required. For about six months, month after month, I pretended to be content with living at Grandma's during my visits with Ms. B.; However, this particular day was different. Overwhelmed with life as it was, I couldn't continue to hold this secret. Ms. B and I were alone in the living room, sitting at the table, while Grandma was upstairs in her room. Ms. B initiated the conversation with, "So Meena, what's been going on?" and I burst into tears. Not sure what was to come next, Ms. B asked, "Meena, are you okay? What's wrong?"

With my face in my hands, I whimpered softly, "He-He rapes me," not to alert Grandma upstairs.

Ms. B responded gently, moving my hands from my face and lifting my head to make eye contact. "Who hurts you, Meena?"

187

I continued to cry, my head down, twiddling my fingers. "Her son, Uncle P. He comes into my room at night when I am sleep and rapes me."

Ms. B exhaled as if she were holding her breath during the entire conversation. Her shoulders slumped down, and she wrapped her arms around me, hugging me tight, and whispered, "I'm going to get you out of here" in my ear. I didn't expect things to happen so quickly, but they escalated when Ms. B made the first phone call.

After Ms. B's first phone call, she began asking me questions. *Reflecting on this experience, I am genuinely grateful for how swiftly Ms. B took action. It demonstrated her genuine concern and commitment to my well-being. Thank you, Ms. B!*

"Is Uncle P in the house now?" she asked.

"No, he isn't here yet. He visits every day, so I'm sure he'll be here soon," I replied, clearing my throat, and wiping my eyes. Ms. B got up from the table to make another phone call, and as she spoke, I found myself wondering about the conversation that was taking place on the other end of the line. I started to feel bad for telling my secret. *Grandma is going to be upset with me, isn't she?*

What is going to happen? I shouldn't have said anything; these intrusive thoughts flooded my mind, and I couldn't hold back the tears any longer.

"Don't worry, Tameena," Ms. B said, pulling the phone down from her ear across her body, before putting the phone back to her ear. "Everything is going to be alright." When she hung up the phone, she returned to the table and sat in front of me to continue the uncomfortable conversation.

"I know this is a lot for you to explain right now, but I need you to do the best you can so I can get as much information as possible to help you," Ms. B explained.

"What is going to happen to me Ms. B?" I asked in fear.

"We are looking into finding another home for you, where you will be safe." she responded.

As Ms. B finished her sentence, Grandma came down the stairs, unaware of what was to come. When she saw my face and the tears that fell from my eyes, she asked what was wrong, and all hell broke loose.

Ms. B ordered me to go upstairs and grab as many things as I could. As I got up from the table to head towards the stairs, Ms. B started the dreaded conversation. "Ms. Martry, I am going to have to take Tameena with me. Your family is officially under investigation for the alleged sexual abuse of Tameena by your son Paul," she explained. I had just passed Grandma and walked to the bottom of the stairs, attempting to sprint up the steps so I didn't have to witness her reaction, but unfortunately, I caught a quick glimpse of it anyway midway up the stairs.

She turned to me and asked, "T-T-Tameena, how c-c-could you do this t-t-to me?" she stuttered softly with disappointment.

Before I could respond, Ms. B interrupted, "Tameena, go and grab your things quickly," reordering me and addressing Grandma next. "Ms. Martry, this is a matter that will have to be settled in court. I followed Ms. B's instructions, rushing up the stairs in tears, my mind filled with worry about what she meant by "a matter in court." Uncertain of the statement, I quickly grabbed whatever I could. This was not a planned move so I wasn't given anything to store my belongings, no trash bags, just my hands. As I got to my room to pick a few things, I paused when I overheard, "Sh-sh-she is a liar, j-j-just like her s-s-sister, and I don't w-w-want her here," Grandma yelled angrily, and what seemed purposefully for me to hear.

Everything I gathered in my arms slipped through my hands, falling to the floor. I raced to the top of the stairs, unable to contain the rage I felt forming inside of me. I yelled back, "My sister did not lie! You didn't believe her because you didn't like her, you evil old hag!" I blurted out, my words piercing through the dark cloud of tension that hung in the air. After my outburst, I quickly ran to pick up the few outfits that slipped from my hands and my green sheet and threw them across my arm, yelling, "It's all your fault!" from my old room. In a rare moment of vulnerability, anger and tears flashed across my face as I dashed down the stairs shouting, "It's your fault he did this to me!" I could feel the heat of rage coursing through my veins, fueled by pain and betrayal. At the bottom of the stairs, Ms. B intercepted me, forming a barrier between Grandma and me. She ushered me out of the house and into her car. The details of whether she finished her conversation with Grandma are still a blur. All I could recall was the dissonance of my own shouts mingled with Grandma's and the abrupt exit to Ms. B's car. *Here I go again,* I thought. Breaking my silence meant moving into another stranger's house. Unbeknownst to me, I was on the path to finding my voice and embarking on a new life of self-advocacy.

CHAPTER FOURTEEN
MOVING AGAIN

"Tameena, are you familiar with Respite Care?" Ms. B asked as she drove me to another place to live.

"Yes," my tone agitated and flat.

"I am going to have to take you to a family, just until we can find you a new foster home."

"I HATE THIS!" I yelled, scaring Ms. B while driving. Ms. B's eyes widened in surprise, and her hands tightened on the steering wheel as my outburst startled her. The car swerved, causing me to jolt side to side in the back seat. She pulled over and parked the car to the right of the curb to get herself together.

"Tameena, I know this is a lot for you to handle, but you have to remain calm, at least while I'm driving. We could've gotten into an accident."

"I am sorry; I'm just so tired of moving from place to place. I don't want to keep doing this. It's not fair."

"I truly understand how you feel Tameena, but we have to get you somewhere to sleep tonight. It may only take a few days before we can find you a new foster home."

Feeling helpless, I couldn't help but think about and accept how little control I had over my life at this point. One minute I was in one house being physically abused by my mother and sister. Then moved to another house to be sexually abused, to another house where the adult just didn't want me there. Moving from place to place had taken a toll on my mind and my body and I just wanted it to stop. As Ms. B continued to talk and explain my situation, I stared out of the window, my mind in a cyclone of thoughts. Silence fell between us for the rest of the ride to the next home.

We arrived at a house in Southwest Philadelphia where a middle-aged woman named Ms. Whitney lived. She seemed pleasant and welcoming. Ms. Whitney invited us into her home, giving me a tour and showing me where I would sleep. Ms. B reminded me that it would only be a short stay, as she would return to take me to my new foster home. Ms. Whitney's house was clean and inviting, and she proved to be a great cook. She prepared breakfast, lunch, and dinner daily, attempting to encourage me and assure me that life would improve with time. Unfortunately, I struggled to absorb her positive words, given my past experiences of disappointment. I was grateful for her kindness; I thanked her.

True to Ms. B's words, my stay with Ms. Whitney lasted only two days before a new foster home became available. The transition began with a phone call to Ms. Whitney, and soon, Ms. B arrived to pick me up. I expressed my gratitude to Ms. Whitney and left with Ms. B, riding the uncertain horizon of yet another foster home.

I got into the car with Ms. B and she began telling me about my new foster parent.

"Tameena, I think this is going to be a good fit for you. Ms. Joanne is going to be your new foster parent. She is up in age, but she is very kind, and there's another foster child there that you can get along with." Ms. B explained.

"How do you know I will get along with her? What if she doesn't like me and treats me mean because I'm new to the home?" I responded.

"I don't think that will happen. Listen Tameena, I know you have been treated unfairly, but you must give this home a chance. If anything happens between you and the other child in her home, let Ms. Joanne know, and she will let me know."

"Ok, I hope I don't have to beat her up, because I will." I said nonchalantly, glaring out of the window.

Ms. B just nodded her head, saying "Let's just cross that bridge when we get there."

Ms. B and I pulled up to a row house in Mt. Airy, PA. The neighborhood looked clean and quiet. We approached the house, rang the doorbell, and a short elderly woman came to the door. *This lady is old*, I thought to myself. Ms. Joanne was about 5 feet tall; she had a little hunchback, and she walked slowly. She looked fly though, her hair was done in a fresh short pixie cut, and her nails looked like she had just come from the nail salon.

"Hi there, come on in, take your shoes off at the door please," she spoke in her shaking squeaky voice.

"Hi Ms. Joanne, this is Tameena. Thank you so much for opening up your home to another child." Ms. B said gratefully.

"Hi Ms. Joanne." I waved.

"You are a beautiful young lady." Ms. Joanne praised.

"Thank you." I giggled shyly.

Ms. Joanne called for her other foster child to come down to meet me, and down came Leah–a fair-skinned girl with her face twisted up, annoyed she had to leave her room.

"Hi, I'm Leah," the girl introduced herself with no emotion in her face or voice.

"Hi, I'm Meena." I responded in my I don't care voice.

It all felt like deja vu. Ms. Joanne gave me a tour of the house, showed me to my room. It was a three-bedroom house, and I had the smallest room of them all. The room was very narrow in width, maybe measuring about 8 feet wide and about 15 feet long. When I walked into the room, there was a bed against the left wall and nothing on the right. There was no space to put anything on the right side of the wall. It was my walking space. Ahead of me against the back wall was a window, and the dresser was against the same wall under the window. *Not that I was ungrateful or anything, but it was a small room.* After the tour of my room, as always, Ms. B left me to live with another stranger. This was a routine that I was tired of following, but I had to go with it. I was determined to make the best out of my situation.

Ms. Joanne kept a clean house, and it was quiet for the most part. She had a light cream carpet all through the house, with a plastic runner from the door to the kitchen. Ms. Joanne wore slippers around the house, careful not to dirty the carpet. The furniture was cream, with wooden trimming, and very clean. When she washed dishes, she wore gloves so that she didn't mess up her fingernails. Ms. Joanne wasn't a good cook, but she cooked at least two meals a day. Leah tried to cook a little as well, but not much. For some reason, Ms. Joanne's ice from her freezer smelled like fish and trash juice; *her ice actually tasted like the smell of fish and trash juice, if you understand what I am saying*. I wasn't home much anyway because of my attendance with school, after school extracurricular activities, and working, so the lack of good food, and smelly ice didn't affect me too much.

The lengthy commute from home to school compelled me to leave two hours earlier than necessary and return home two hours later than required. I lived across town, far from everything I knew, my church, my friends, and my high school. Living in Mt. Airy and being away from what I knew as normalcy, added to the frustration of being in foster care. Although I moved to a different area of the city, I continued the same routine at the same places in Southwest and West Philadelphia. I still attended West Philadelphia High School, *SPEED BOYZ!!,* which was an hour and a half away, riding the bus from my new foster home. Despite all of this, living with Ms. Joanne wasn't horrible, but there was something about her that bothered me.

Living with Ms. Joanne wasn't too bad, but me going to school functions after school and church functions made Ms. Joanne a little mad for some reason. She would always complain about me being out so late even when I was coming home from church functions. I was at church almost every night for something and did reach home around 9 or 10 p.m. each night, but she made it seem like I was out partying in the streets, *been there and done that, and this time I was really searching for Jesus.* Ms. Joanne would say things like, "Those God people keeping you out all late. I don't see how you believe in that stuff." She would make up these outrageous curfew times so that I wouldn't be able to go to church, without telling me I couldn't go to church. Ms. Joanne was no Christian like myself, and neither was Leah. Sometimes Leah would say things like "You're always at church. Don't you want to do something fun?" As if she knew what fun was, she stayed under her boyfriend who kept breaking up with her all the time. I really didn't like it when Ms. Joanne and Leah talked about me going to church with "God people," but I didn't say anything to them about it. I just continued to attend my church. I didn't have to worry about being hurt by any men in her family. She really didn't have that many family members visit her except for her daughter and granddaughter. Ms. Joanne's house was easy to bear.

CHAPTER FIFTEEN
A BLAST FROM THE PAST

This one day in high school, someone from my past showed up. It took me by surprise; I never thought I would run into him again. It was Rob from the block in North Philly. Rob and I had an entanglement back when Lyfe was pimping me out. Seeing him flooded my mind with nasty, embarrassing, and now funny flashbacks. Those were funny flashbacks. When Lyfe sold me to Rob one day, he didn't know what to do. When he finally got it, he thought he was doing something with his little wee-wee, but he wasn't. To this day, I still don't count him as my first. Looking at him now, I could tell it wasn't a little wee-wee anymore. At least I hoped not, (ooh, this page just got hot as I was writing, I feel like you guys are judging me right now. Don't judge me, love me, okay? There is somebody reading this that remembers Rob and thought about his little wee-wee). The not-so-funny flashbacks that came to mind were when Lyfe would blackmail me with a beating from my mother, and she had Rob touch me inappropriately for a few dollars, and she didn't even give me any money; *that was rude of her, and I was no prostitot (young prostitute) or anything. How is she gonna get money for something I did and not break me off?* Another time Lyfe tried to get me to suck Rob's penis, but I bossed up and said no, and the time we had sex with his little wee-wee — those flashbacks I thought were erased from my mind came flooding back as soon as I saw him.

Apparently, you can't stop flashbacks from the past. Still, you can determine what you want to do with those flashbacks, and at this moment, I could remember everything that happened to me, and be embarrassed every time I see him, or I could either act like nothing ever happened and move on. I'd like to believe that in my young teenage mind, I was choosing to leave the past behind and move forward in life. As nerve-wracking as it was to see Rob, I must admit that it was nice seeing someone that I was familiar with, someone who knew me- the old me. I saw Rob walking through the halls of my high school.

When he saw me, he yelled, "Meena, you go here?" as he walked over to me, looking at me up and down.

I responded, "Oh my goodness, Rob, yeah, it's me!" as we hugged each other.

"Wow, look at you!" He said, holding my hand and twirling me around as if we used to be old lovers, best friends, or something.

"It's me!" I smiled as I allowed him to twirl me in a circle before letting go of his hand.

I know he was checking me out; I wasn't that bony, scrawny little girl he once knew six years ago. Don't get me wrong, I was still thin; but getting thick in all the right places. We started to walk the halls as he asked me about my sisters and told me about my mother and how she was still drinking and partying. We couldn't talk much because we had to go to our separate classes until we met up at lunch, but it was nice to see Rob.

I went to class, and my mind started to play tricks on me. Thoughts crept into my head about Rob and that somehow, he would embarrass me in front of my friends and any friends he would make. I thought, *what if he tells the boys what we used to do on the block? What if he tells them how he paid my sister to have sex with me and stuff? Then everyone will be looking at me like I'm a whore, and the*

203

boys will start treating me like a whore. What if Yani found out? She wouldn't want to be my friend anymore; I can't lose my best friend. Man, my thoughts had me going crazy. I was so scared, so embarrassed, and I didn't know what was going to happen next. At first, I was so excited- *more surprised than excited* to see Rob, and was looking forward to lunch, but then I became so anxious and afraid. I felt like the 10-year-old girl who didn't speak up for herself six years ago all over again. Then finally a calm came over me, and I was reminded of who Rob was six years ago. He was timid like me, a nice person doing the wrong thing, but still a kind-hearted person. Maybe he wouldn't do that to me because that wasn't how I remembered him to be, I thought. Shoot, if push came to shove and he tried to play me, I would let everyone know about his little wee-wee and tell how he didn't know how to use it; I would capitalize on this, I thought. Besides, he knows about these hands and how they work, especially on boys. He was there when I whipped Meek's ass for knocking Sophie down the stairs back on the block. I don't think he wants this smoke, but it's been a while, and he might think I'm soft now. Time will tell what will happen next. At this point, lunch was about to start, and I needed to be ready for whatever was going to happen.

The bell rang, and it was lunchtime, and time to see if my life was going to turn upside down or if Rob was going to leave my past in the closet. Yani and I left class and walked into the lunchroom. Rob was already in the lunchroom talking with a bunch of boys whom I knew, and some I didn't really know that well. I was so nervous, my stomach started to do flips. I walked to get my lunch and sat at the table with Yani and our friends to chat it up and talk about people. That's what we did a lot. For us not to be popular, we sure did make fun of everybody, even the popular kids. This day it was hard for me to focus on making fun of people, because I had my own imposter syndrome situation going on that I needed not to come to light. Instead of listening to my friends laugh and have fun, I had my eyes glued on Rob, trying to read his lips, and trying to see if he was looking in my direction because that would mean he was talking about me.

Yani nudged me, saying, "Meena, what's up with you? Are you okay? Who are you looking at?"

"Me, oh, nobody I thought I saw someone who looked familiar; ha-ha-ha, y'all crazy," I said, pretending to hear what they were talking and laughing about. I couldn't tell Yani what was happening, one because it was embarrassing and two because she would ask too many questions. Yani would stop me mid-sentence to ask questions before I could finish the sentence because she had to know every single detail, but I wasn't ready to expose myself and explain this kind of information. As I stared Rob up and down, I noticed he had an ankle monitor from the Juvenile Justice Center (juvie) on his left ankle, and I needed to know the reason he was in juvie. I needed to know how he got caught up; he was one of the good ones. He must have been hanging around the wrong crowd or something, but I was going to find out.

Rob never came over to me at lunch, and neither did I to him because I didn't want to bring too much attention to us. He stayed talking and hanging out with the boys, and I stayed at the table with Yani and our friends. I was thinking of how I was going to somehow wait around the lunchroom to talk to him before going to my next class without Yani noticing. Very discreetly, I continued to make glances at Rob until his eyes met mine. I motioned by nodding my head to the right for him to meet me outside of the lunchroom. I told Yani I was going to the bathroom really quick and that I would be right back, and I left the lunchroom. Rob nodded back to make sure I was talking to him before he started to leave the lunchroom.

He met me in the hallway, and I asked, "So what's with the ankle bracelet?"

He responded, "Nah, it's nothing; I just got in a little trouble on the block, but I won't be here for long because I will be going back to Norf (North Philly) soon."

"Rob, you have always been the better person out of Slim and Meek. What little trouble?" I asked as if he owed me an explanation. I don't even know why I felt the need to know his business, but I guess I felt like he was the only one in the school who knew me, so I felt comfortable asking.

"Meena, I got caught with some weed and a gun on me, that's all," he said with a stupid smirk on his face.

All I could do was look at him and wonder why, but I decided to mind my own business. I remember what it was like to do stupid things for stupid or survival reasons, so I left it alone.

"Well, take care of yourself out in these streets," I told him as I walked back into the lunchroom.

"You take care of yourself," he responded, watching me walk away.

I went back into the cafeteria for the last few minutes of lunch. Rob had only attended West Philly High for that week, and then he stopped showing up.

CHAPTER SIXTEEN
THE LONGEST BUS RIDE EVER

It was the Longest Bus Ride Ever!!, or just another day to be taken advantage of by a complete stranger. Growing up in Philadelphia, everyone traveled using SEPTA, at least anyone who didn't have a car or anyone who had to walk over a mile. SEPTA wasn't always the most pleasant or enjoyable experience. Aside from being able to travel alone, it got me from point A to point B quicker than walking. In the front of the bus, there were seats labeled for the physically disabled or elderly people, so they didn't have to walk so far to the back of the bus. Many times, people sat there and ignored the sign, even when the individuals it was designed for entered the bus. I admit that sometimes I sat at the front of the bus, especially when I wasn't familiar with where I was going or what stop I was going to get off, but when I saw someone handicapped arrive on the bus, I would move so that they would be able to sit, and I would stand instead. Although my mother had her issues in raising her children, she made sure we had manners and that we were respectful to our elders. Sometimes I would hear young people telling senior citizens, "You better walk your old self to the back of the bus, your feet not broke," on a crowded bus.

My siblings and I were raised to say "yes, ma'am" and "no, ma'am," "yes, sir" and "no, sir" to any adult. Every time I encountered the elderly, it was yet another reminder of who I was and who I originally came from. On the bus, there would be people sitting and standing, people holding onto the metal vertical and horizontal poles at the top of the bus. Most of the time, I would be squeezed between two strangers who sometimes smelled good, and sometimes they didn't smell so good.

At times, because the bus was packed to capacity, some bus drivers would just ride past designated stops, which made waiting on the bus sometimes a major problem, especially if the bus rode right past you. Although each bus had its own schedule, most of the time buses would show up late, sometimes even a whole hour late. SEPTA was not always a reliable source of transportation if you wanted to get anywhere on time. Riding the bus was always uncomfortable, but I needed to take it to get to and from school, church, and friends' houses — the very few friends' houses who later became family.

One nice spring day, I was on my way home from school. I boarded the 119 bus that took me from 69th Street to Broad and Olney. I was doing my regular long commute; surprisingly, I had no worries in my head at the time. It was always hard to find a seat where I could sit alone, but today I spotted two empty seats right next to each other. The seat was in the back of the bus. I had to walk by lots of people who I thought were staring at me as I took the dreadfully long walk, which was only about six feet away from the seat I'd claimed with my eyes. As I sat on the left side of the bus in the left seat, leaving the left seat vacant. I gazed out of the window mindlessly, enjoying the ride home. The bus came to a stop, and passengers began to board the bus. A man, who was about 5'5", brown skinned, and wearing a white T-shirt with blue denim shorts, came and sat next to me. I continued to look out the window, waiting for my stop to come, which was only a few blocks away. I was wearing a nice white T-shirt with hearts on it and a blue denim skirt that was about to the top of my knee standing, but when sitting it raised a little higher. My skirt had a small split about 2 inches high right in the front middle of my skirt. It was a good day to dress up and enjoy the breeze of spring. Suddenly, the hands of my neighbor passenger started caressing my right leg by moving his hand up and down. By the time it clicked what was happening, my first reaction was to move his hand and attempt to change my seat. As I moved his hand, saying, "Excuse me!" He gave me a look. When I attempted to get up to change my seat, he pulled out a small knife from his pocket, pointing it low at me, and gesturing for me to sit down. Out of fear, I sat down, not knowing what to do or say; I was panicking but not outwardly. The only thing I could think of was to let my neighbor passenger continue to rub my legs. I tightened my knees together preventing his hand from going any higher, but then he pinched my leg, making me loosen the grip of my closed legs. His hands went up my skirt. His fingers first caressed my thighs as he was trying to reach higher. I noticed he couldn't quite reach my vagina without dislocating his shoulder from the position where he was sitting, which was a good thing. I felt like I could handle this, that he would give up and I would get off soon at my stop. As soon as I thought that the passenger moved his hand from under my skirt and reached into the top of my skirt, pushing me back so he could shimmy his hand right into my skirt. I squirmed a little to make it hard for him, but he gave me this look of death. It was a dangerous and dark look that I didn't want to explore, so I let him continue to struggle to get in my skirt until he succeeded. His nasty feeling, long slinky fingers slipped through my jean skirt, without even unbuttoning the button, through my panties, and touching my vagina. He then pinched my thighs again, forcing me to open my legs more because I was clenching my thighs tight. *I was used to being pinched by Grandma when she used to pinch me in the church to get my attention or for me to stop doing something.* Before I knew it, his fingers were in my vagina. Swerving from side to side and in and out. I sat there, embarrassed of myself and of everyone on the bus. To me, it felt like everyone saw and thought of me as the dirty, nasty hoe. I sat with tears in my eyes, just wondering, *why me? Why does this continue to happen to me? Is there a sign on me that says, "take me," "available," "easy," or even "scared"*? I was so afraid that I just let him take advantage of me. I was finally living up to the names my mother used to call me; I was a slutty girl, a hussy who just let boys have their way with me. The bus traveled for a few blocks, and of course, I missed my stop. We rode until he was finished with me. I just wished someone could see what was happening and care enough to say something about it, but maybe no one saw, maybe no one cared, or maybe I was just another slutty girl being nasty on the bus. When my neighbor passenger was finished, he released his fingers from inside of me, smelled them, and then wiped his hands off on my skirt. I was so disgusted with myself and with him; I couldn't even look at him. Before he left, he pulled out his knife again, as if to remind me of what could happen if I decided to say or do anything. He folded his little knife and put it back in his pocket. He then got up, pulled the yellow cord to signal "next stop," and walked to the front of the bus to get off at the next stop. He waited to exit the bus as if nothing had ever happened. When the bus came to a complete stop, my neighbor passenger looked back at me, smiled, and got off the bus. I couldn't stand to look at him out of fear of him telling me to follow him, so I took one look to see if he was getting off the bus and quickly put my head down in fear and disgust.

The neighbor passenger didn't even have to say a word to me, and he was able to have his way with me. I thought of myself as cheap, nasty, and shallow; although I thought there was nothing I could do, my mind began to race with things I should have done. *Why can't I stick up for myself? Why do I just let people walk all over me?* I thought to myself. The reality was that I never stood up for myself for anything; fear kept me from standing up for myself. This was just another, not so good, perk I'd inherited from my mother. *Maybe I should have screamed and yelled, but then he would have stabbed me with the shank. I should have just tried to move my seat again, but then he would have stabbed me with the shank. I should have kicked his ass, but then he would have stabbed me with the shank.* All these scenarios played in my head, but the result was always the same, which drove my fear of moving, so I had to let him have his way. Next thing I knew, it was the last stop and everyone was off the bus except the bus driver and myself. "Excuse me, young lady, this is the last stop," the bus driver said. I just looked at him saying, "I'm not a young lady" with tears in my eyes and got off the bus. Now this wasn't the first time I missed my stop and ended up at the last stop before. I would fall asleep after a long day of school, volleyball practice, and choir practice, and then finally travel home on a trolley, the El, and then the bus. On those occasions, I would stay on the bus and wait for the bus to turn around to go the opposite way, but this time I couldn't bear to be alone on the bus with another male because of the fear of what could happen. I thought for sure there was something on me labeled for men to see and explore. Although I felt so bad and clueless, I said to myself that, whatever just happened, I had to shake it off. I gave into the fact that this is what happens, and life goes on. I wiped my eyes, my nose and went to the store to get a bottle of water. I drank some water, then I went to the bathroom in a Dunkin' Donuts and washed myself with the bottle of water and paper towels. It wasn't easy to wash in a public bathroom, not knowing if customers would walk in at any time. The bathroom had three stalls and two sinks in front of the bathroom. I would have to go in the bathroom and sit on the toilet to pour the water between my legs, letting the water spill into the toilet as I used paper towels to wipe myself. When I ran out of water, I would peek out of the stall to see if anyone was out at the sinks; so, I could refill my bottle of water. I would creep out of the stall with my pants down. I repeated this process around three times. As I scrubbed my wet and disgusted vagina, I cried again. "Pull yourself together, this is life now, so suck it up," is what I told myself. I cleaned myself up, left Dunkin' Donuts, and got on the next bus back home. That was the longest ride home ever; I was so tired, disgusted, and afraid all at the same time. I was nauseous at the thought of my day, but I still had to move on. On the way home, I thought about if I was going to tell anyone about what I just experienced. *Should I tell my Ms. Joanne what happened; would she care?* along with lots of other things that popped into my head. Suddenly, my bus stop came up and I exited the bus.

I exited the bus and walked the longest, loneliest two blocks home ever. During the walk, I thought every man, boy, or guy period was looking at me in a nasty way. I just started to walk fast with my head down, eager to be inside and away from the open and vulnerable world. Finally, I reached home, not speaking to anyone, brushed past my foster parent, my foster sister, and went straight to my room to grab a towel, then straight into the bathroom to take a proper and well-deserved shower. My shower was about twenty-five minutes around that time. Ms. Joanne yelled, "Get out of the shower and stop wasting my water." *If she only knew why I was taking this long shower, maybe she wouldn't be so stingy with her water today or would she. I seem to be the blame for everything that happens to me,* I thought. When my shower ended, I put on my night clothes and went straight to bed. It was only about 4:30 p.m. but I was ready for this day to end already. As I attempted to sleep, those thoughts of should've, would've, could've's, bombarded my mind. I began to beat myself up for allowing such things to happen to me, questioning, *was it my fault? Was it what I wore? Did I have my legs closed enough?* I couldn't sleep because all of what was going on in my head had gotten the best of me. I wanted to end it all; I wanted to die. I couldn't stand the thought of this happening to me again. It was all too much to ponder; I knew I wasn't strong enough to cut my wrists or hang myself; it would hurt too much. Instead, I walked to the bathroom, grabbed a bottle of Advil, ran the water, and popped pills. I threw back a few pills at a time, then drank some water, and repeated the same process about four times. I had to have taken about 20 Advils; I thought I would die in my sleep and never wake up, never having to deal with this pain again. I walked back to my room, closed my door, and plopped down on my bed, staring at the ceiling until I fell asleep. Well, fool on me because of course I didn't die, but instead was left with a terrible headache; my head was spinning, and so was the room. I was so nauseous; I climbed out of bed, walked down the hall holding my head, and threw up in the bathroom sink. It was a close call; I almost threw up all over the floor, but I made it to the sink first and then to the toilet. Leah asked me "Uh, are you ok? Are you pregnant or something?" in her flat tone. *Wouldn't you like that,* I thought, but I didn't respond; I couldn't respond. I was so angry that I was alive and in so much pain; I could barely see. I flushed the toilet, washed my face and hands, left the bathroom, and went to my room to go to sleep. Still hoping I would not wake up again, never wanting to relive this day ever, not in a dream, a conversation, not even a thought. After a few interruptions of getting up and throwing up throughout the night, I finally fell asleep, and to my surprise, I woke up again the next morning — alive.

CHAPTER SEVENTEEN
SHE KICKING ME OUT!

The day came when I got bad news, news that shook my world back up into millions of pieces. I was alone at home, Ms. Joanne was out getting her hair and nails done, *she got her hair and nails done every week,* and Leah was at work. There was an unexpected ring at the door; it was my social worker, Ms. Bridge. She came to visit me in July, a month after I graduated from high school.

She sat me down at the living room table and said, "So, have you found a place to live?"

Confused, I answered, "What do you mean? I live here."

"She didn't tell you?" Ms. Bridge asked.

I responded, "No, tell me what?

"Ms. Joanne said she would not be able to take care of you anymore," Ms. Bridge explained.

I immediately got upset in my head as to why. Time stopped for a minute as I contemplated if I should ask the question "Why?" aloud. Finally, I just came out with it.

"Why didn't she tell me? How she just gonna put us out on the streets without telling us?" I said with an attitude, assuming Leah had to leave as well. I was steaming, but I was still calm.

Ms. Bridge answered, "Well actually, Leah is staying; she just needs you to leave by the end of the month."

"Are you kidding me; that's only about two weeks away." At this point, my blood was boiling with anger, fear, and shame.

"I knew she didn't like me yo; I never did anything to her. I'm barely here; all I do is sleep here. I ain't do nothing to her; she never liked me!" I ranted.

I honestly believed that Ms. Joanne didn't like me because I went to church a lot. She used to act funny toward me when I would come back from church and say things like, "What did your God people say today?" or "How many days do you have to go to church? It's like you live at church; the church sees you more than I do," she'd say with an attitude. She was right; I basically lived at church because I was so invested in the ministries. I was a part: singing in the choir, participating in the praise team, dancing in the dance ministry, and going to bible study. I loved my church and the people who made me feel welcomed and loved by God.

"That's not it, Tameena, she just can't afford to keep you anymore," Ms. Bridge said calmly.

"Oh, so it's about money. I'll be turning 18 soon, and she won't be getting a check for me anymore!" I continued to rant, not really knowing if what I was saying was even a fact.

"We have to find a place for you to live. You have two options here. The first option is, you could be put in another foster home, although it would be hard because you are aging out of foster care soon *which really means, no one wants a teenager as a foster child*. The second option is you can find a place to live on your own." She said it so casually, as if I'd been planning to move out for some time now, and had enough money saved up to just up and move. I said all this in my head, but she must have heard my mind speaking and said, "I can see you are upset. I'm sorry for this outcome, but you have two weeks to decide. I will be back in two weeks to pick you up," as she gathered her things and headed out the door.

I was just so undone that I couldn't even say goodbye to her when she left. I was enraged with fear, but I kept it together. I have always held my anger in until I couldn't hold it anymore, until the point of explosion. Even though this day gave me a reason to explode in total combustion, I couldn't. I went back into survivor mode. I had a pity party for myself after Ms. Bridge left. I went to my room, laid across my made-up bed with all my clothes and sneakers on, and cried. Though I was alone in the house, I buried my face in the pillow so no one could hear me cry; not even my shame could hear me. Time and time again, I found myself back at zero. Every time I finally got comfortable somewhere, I was uprooted and moved somewhere else. My mind raced with negative thoughts of trashing the house, blowing it up, or committing suicide. Before my brain could process anything else, BOOM, I exploded, and I let out a big scream! Furiously, I banged my head back and forth on my pillow, face down. I jumped up out of bed, yelling and screaming, "I hate myself! I hate myself! Why was I even born?" I stripped the sheets and pillow off my bed with my two hands, banging them up against the wall. I screamed, "I hate this place!" while pacing the length of the room, pulling out every wooden drawer, and throwing them to the floor. It was like I blacked out for a few minutes. I remember being so tired; that I just fell to the floor crying, asking myself, *what did I do now? Why am I always messing up and making people hate me? Every time I open my mouth about something, it backfires on me and causes me to lose people.* Unable to see clearly through the tears in my eyes, I looked around at the mess I had made, and thought, *see, I always make a mess out of things.* Wiping my eyes with the back of my hand and the bottom of my shirt, I stood up and started cleaning up my mess. Besides, I didn't want Ms. Joanne coming home, and seeing this mess; it would just give her a more legitimate reason as to why she was kicking me out. As I write this, it seems that moment was a bit bipolar. I went from raging to being unbothered, and I remained calm while I was cleaning. Come to think of it, cleaning was my happy place, a way to destress. When I lived with my mother, cleaning was a safety net. If I was cleaning, I wasn't being beaten. At Grandma's house, cleaning made me feel good and accomplished, and now, cleaning is a stress reliever. As I concentrate on cleaning, it allows me to think clearly. I went into survival mode; I still thought about the situation, but I was thinking more of solutions like getting a job to make money and getting my own place. One thing I knew was that I didn't want to go to another foster home, learn a new family, and start all over again. I didn't want that for myself, except I just didn't know where to start, especially because I didn't have a job at the time.

Not too long before Ms. Bridge's visit, I had just quit my job at Walmart in South Philly. The customers were rude and ghetto. It wasn't a good fit for me; I saw myself getting fired for cursing somebody out or punching a customer in the face. So, I did the honor of letting myself go, and I quit. One day while working at the cash register, a customer was being so rude, and put their money on the conveyor belt instead of in my hand. That was so rude to me, at least you can put the money in my hand. I had my hands out for you to put the money in my hand. So, I acted like I didn't see them put the money on the conveyor belt, and I let it get stuck. A customer got mad at me because her dollar bill got stuck in the belt, to which I replied, "Ma'am, I didn't see it. My hand was out for you to hand me the money." She was getting smart, and I just took it all in. Other stuff was happening too, and it was just too much for me. I was getting close to my breaking point. When it was time for me to go on break, I took a long break, so long that I haven't been back since. Yani called me on my cell, telling me the manager was asking for me. They were calling my name on the loudspeaker and everything.

"Girl, where you at? They are calling for you," Yani whispered.

"Girl, I'm home, I quit." I told her, cracking up.

We both burst out laughing. I just couldn't do it, but unbeknownst to me, I was about to be homeless. I would have sucked it up to survive. I would have saved all the money I had earned in middle school and high school, so at least I would have used it to pay for a hotel or studio apartment. Anyway, I started thinking of ways I could help myself. The crazy thing is, I never considered asking anyone for help. I felt I was on my own and didn't bother to mention it to anyone for a while.

About a week later, my friends from church, Jinniyah and Tattiana, came over. We were all sitting in the basement while Ms. Joanne was upstairs in the kitchen "cooking," *Ms. Joanne was not a good cook.* During our conversation, the topic of college came up.

Jinniyah asked, "So, are you excited about going to college?"

"Yeah, I guess," I responded, not sure if I was going or not. There was just too much going on at the time.

"Why do you sound like you don't want to go? College is going to be fun; you get to go to parties and meet guys!" Tattiana said.

"Yeah, girl, and you will be living on your own until you have to come home for breaks and stuff!" Jinniyah added.

All this sounded great, but I couldn't see past my current situation that neither of them knew about. *Should I tell them what was going on? No, they will judge you and know that you will be homeless. They wouldn't be able to help me anyway; at this point, it doesn't even matter, and I don't care,* I thought.

"Ms. Joanne is kicking me out!" I blurted.

"What you mean she kicking you out?" Jinniyah asked.

"What! How she just gonna kick you out? Did something happen?" Tattiana asked.

"Nothing happened, it's about money; she told my social worker that she can't afford to take care of me anymore. I can stay here one more week until I go to college, but I won't have anywhere to live during the breaks." I explained.

"I never liked her; that's why her ICE NASTY AND STANK!" Jinniyah yelled so Ms. Joanne could hear upstairs.

Jinniyah was always good at breaking the ice- *not Ms. Joanne's ice, you know what I mean,* and making people laugh. Tattiana and I started cracking up laughing because this was a fact. Jinniyah, Tattiana and I, continued our conversation about me being homeless during the college breaks and Jinniyah asked, "You want to live with me?"

"Ah, I guess. I don't know if I can," I responded hesitantly. While Jinniyah and I were talking, I noticed that Tattiana had made a phone call; "Hello Mom, can Tameena come live with us? Ms. Joanne is kicking her out for no reason." Jinniyah and I looked at

Tattiana wondering when she called, because we didn't even finish our conversation.

"My mom said you can live with us!" Tattiana said excitedly.

"Dang, girl. I was asking her to live with me. I didn't even get a chance to finish my sentence," Jinniyah laughed.

I was kind of glad I didn't have to choose whose house to go to because Tattiana had settled the matter once she called her mom. It didn't really matter at the moment because Jinniyah and Tattiana are first cousins who were like sisters. To be with one was to be with both, and I loved hanging around them and their family.

"Oh, my goodness, are you serious? She's just gonna take me in like that?" I asked surprisedly.

"For real, for real, we hang out all the time; you're like family anyway. Now you can live with us, and we can be a real family," Tattitana said.

"True!" Jinniyah added as we hugged it out in a circle.

I was so moved by the sentiments of Tattiana's actions and Jinniyah's attempt to get me to live with her that I responded quickly, and answered, "Yes, I guess I'm going to come and live with you! Thank you so much!!"

To be honest, I wasn't home much anyway. After daily volleyball practice, Monday night praise and worship rehearsal, Tuesday night dance rehearsal, Wednesday night Bible study, Thursday night choir rehearsal, and some Friday night youth activities, I was just getting home to sleep, and most of the time, I stayed with my Aunt Sandrine on the weekends so that I could hang out with Jinniyah and Tattiana anyway. It was the principle of you not doing what you're supposed to do for me and then getting called out on your bluff, then kicking me out as if it was all my fault but moving out of Ms. Joanne's house turned out to be a blessing to me. Before the end of the week, I was all moved out of Ms. Joanne's house and into Tattiana's house.

When I left Ms. Joanne's house, I was under the impression that she was kicking me out because she couldn't afford to take care of me with the little money she was getting from the agency, but later (20 years later) learned that the reason she didn't want me to live with her was because I told the truth about the care I was receiving. A few months before finding out I was getting the boot from Ms. Joanne; Ms. Bridge visited me for a well-being appointment. During our meeting, she asked questions like, "Other than food and shelter, does Ms. Joanne supply you with your basic needs, like clothes, toiletries, and/or allowance?" and I answered honestly with "No, no, and no," not understanding that Ms. Joanne was supposed to be supplying me with these things. I explained to Ms. Bridge that I had a job and I bought my own clothes, sanitary napkins, and deodorants, and that I didn't need an allowance because I had my own job. Ms. Bridge explained that even though I have a job, Ms. Joanne was still supposed to be supporting me with these things because she was getting paid to do so. Ms. Bridge asked Leah the same questions, and her answers mirrored mine. We didn't try to talk badly about Ms. Joanne; we simply answered questions that were asked of us. After Leah's and my individual meeting with Ms. Bridge, she contacted her supervisor to report her findings of Ms. Joanne not fulfilling her foster parent duties, and an open investigation was opened on Ms. Joanne's behalf. She was asked for monthly receipts of all the things that she bought for us and did not have them to prove her case, so as a result, she kicked me out!

I learned that Ms. Joanne was mainly upset with me because I told the truth first, starting a ripple effect down to Leah telling the truth, and the truth made her look bad. She originally wanted both me and Leah gone, but Leah was able to plead her case and ask for a second chance, but I was not even given the decency of Ms. Joanne or Leah to let me know what was happening. By the time Ms. Bridge came to me with the news, Leah had already known and begged Ms. Joanne to stay without mentioning to me that I was going to be leaving and had kept it secret for two weeks. Leah explained that she didn't know they were asking these questions to get her in trouble, and that although she answered the questions correctly, she didn't know it would have such an impact on Ms. Joanne. Leah literally cried to Ms. Joanne, explaining that she had nowhere else to go and no other family members to turn to, and asked if she could at least stay for a few more months to save up before she moved out. Ms. Joanne agreed, and they both agreed not to put me in the loop. Leah stayed with Ms. Joanne for about two more years after I left until she moved out on her own.

I always struggled with speaking up for myself or speaking out against something that I knew was wrong to protect someone else's feelings. It seemed like every time I got the courage to speak up for myself, I was left with guilt, shame, and being displaced. I was leaving another home for simply speaking out about something that was done to me, in which case I didn't even know I was being neglected financially. Even though there was no fault of my own, I felt responsible for my eviction, and I felt bad that Ms. Joanne felt betrayed by me. If there is one thing, I never wanted to do was to make someone feel betrayed, yet that was all I seemed to do with people who were caring for me. It made me feel like I wasn't worthy of being cared for, and that I should somehow care for myself. I should be alone in the streets to be another statistic about the outcome of children who were in foster care, especially because the agency did not provide me with any resources on how to make it on my own. Although this time, I am glad I spoke up to tell Jinniyah and Tattiana that I was getting kicked out because, without them I may have been on the streets.

I learned that out of the 23,000 children that will age out of foster care, about 20% of those children will become homeless immediately. It is suspected that only 1 out of 2 foster kids will be gainfully employed by the age of 24. Less than 3% of those children may earn a college degree. Statistics go on to show that 7 out of 10 girls will become pregnant by the time they are 21 years of age, and 25% of foster children will suffer from PTSD (National Foster Youth Institute (NFYI)). I didn't know about these statistics when I chose to emancipate myself from the foster care system. Even if I did know about the statistics, I don't know if it would have changed my mind, but I would have at least thought twice about emancipating myself. What I didn't understand back when I made the decision was how there were no resources or information given to me as to how I could care for myself. "When children age out of foster care, they become ineligible to receive state assistance with housing, food, and medical care under the foster care system. The federal government recognized that this, coupled with the fact that foster children typically already suffer ill effects due to the lack of a stable home environment while growing up, was causing newly emancipated young adults to suffer higher rates of substance abuse, mental illness, teen pregnancy, homelessness, and arrests (Housing Assistance for Youth Who Have Aged Out Of Foster Care). I now see that life after foster care was not a priority in the foster care system. There was no formal paperwork for me to sign; it was a verbal agreement that I would be on my own from here on out. It felt like being kicked out of a parent's house for misbehaving. No direction, just leave and figure it out on your own. Although I'm glad I got the chance to move in with my friends. I was moving in with the mindset that everything will be fine if I don't complain about anything because I don't want to betray my friends.

CHAPTER EIGHTEEN
STRANGE ENCOUNTERS

There were times in my life when I had been involved in a few strange encounters with people. Some of these people were complete strangers, and some were people I knew very well. It seemed like I was a magnet for suggestive sexual contacts because I always wound up in situations that I didn't ask for from boys, girls, men, and women.

One strange encounter was when I was living with Grandma after all my sisters left me; I became very close with Stacey. Stacey was Grandma's real granddaughter who lived next door to us with her dad (Grandma's son) Uncle John; *yes, the mother and son lived right next door to each other.* Stacey would often come over to hang with me because Uncle John used Grandma as a babysitter most of the time. We would just talk, and sometimes we would just hang out outside. One day, Stacey came over to Grandma's house while I was sleeping. I was in my bed sleeping when I heard Stacey's voice. She came into the room and said, "Oh, you sleep, I'm gonna just lay next to you," so I looked up at her, and moved over for her to lay next to me. I was lying on my left side with my back facing the door when Stacey came and lay next to me in the spooning position. Girls sleep in the bed together all the time, so I didn't think anything of it, although she was a little close. I was half asleep and just ignored the closeness.

I fell back asleep, which may have been for another half hour or so, and I woke up to a feeling of something poking in the back of me. All my clothes were still on, but it felt like a ball was poking me in my butt area. So many thoughts ran through my mind, *I hope this is not Uncle P behind me,* but it didn't feel like him because the bed wasn't heavy behind me, I wasn't restrained or anything, and most of all, it didn't smell like him. When I turned around, I saw it was still Stacey behind me. She had a balled-up sock, or a few balled up socks, in her pants and was spooned against me, pushing on me like she was a dude or something. "What the fuck are you doing?" I said, angrily pushing her away from me. I pushed her so hard; she almost fell off the bed.

"I'm just playing!" Stacey laughed.

"Don't play with me like that. That shit ain't funny," I said seriously.

"My bad, I didn't know you were going to get that mad," she said, taking the socks out of her pants.

"What made you put socks in your pants anyway?" I questioned, out of curiosity, as to how she thought to do something like that.

"I don't know, I heard about other people in my school doing it to each other, so I thought it would be funny to do it to you," Stacey responded, still chuckling.

I let that go, and we continued to lay next to each other in bed talking and going on about our day.

Stacey didn't know about what I went through at home when I was living with my mother. My older sisters Lyfe and Isabella used to make me get on top of them and move back and forth, humping on them so they could get off, I guess. I'm not going to act like it didn't feel good at times, humping my sisters, but I knew it wasn't right. They were my sisters, and I was too young to be humping anything anyway. It wasn't new to me that people did this, but the whole sock thing was new and a little weird. After that day, Stacey and I continued to hang out with each other. She continued to "play" like that with me, until eventually we started to hump each other sometimes. I knew I shouldn't have done it, but it felt good sometimes. It felt better than having a penis in me, like when I was being raped by Uncle P., I never enjoyed that feeling, but I did enjoy being humped by Stacey. It wasn't like Stacey was that pretty of a girl, but it felt good, so we "played" sometimes. Stacey was the last girl I played with like that, because I thought it was just something to do. It wasn't my sexual orientation or anything. I liked boys, but being raped by Stacey's uncle was too much. Boys weren't on my list of things to "play" with at the time.

Another strange encounter was with a person who was a stranger to me but was related to Grandma; he was from Atlanta, Georgia (ATL). Grandma and I went to visit her sister who lived in ATL. I had never heard of this sister before, nor have I'd ever been to ATL before, and I was so excited to go. It was my first vacation with Grandma, and I felt like I was finally part of her family. We took the train because Grandma did not like to fly, and the bus would have taken too long. When we arrived at her sister's house, we were greeted at the door with hugs and kisses. Her sister Ms. Jean hugged and kissed me like she knew me. Her grandson came to the door to take our luggage, and we all entered the house. Grandma introduced me to Ms. Jean, saying, "Jean, th-th-this is my gr-gr-granddaughter, Tameena; Tameena, th-th-this is your Au-Au-Aunt Jean." I was so surprised that Grandma didn't mention that I was her foster child. She introduced me as her granddaughter, and it made me feel good about myself and gave me a sense of belonging. Maybe Aunt Jean already knew I was her foster child; *I'm sure they've had phone conversations about me.* Either way, I felt good. Aunt Jean responded, "It is so good to finally meet you, Tameena! This is my grandson Jahlil." Jahlil waved, and I waved back. He was fourteen years old, about two years older than me, and looked a little nerdy with his tall, lanky frame and dark-framed glasses. I didn't think we'd talk much because he seemed like a loner, and that was okay with me.

We stayed at Aunt Jean's house for five days. She had a two-bedroom house with a living room and a kitchen. The house wasn't big; it was smaller than Grandma's house. Aunt Jean's room was in the back, Jahlil's bedroom was on the right side of the hallway, and the bathroom was directly across from Jahlil's room. Grandma slept in the bed with her sister, and I slept on an air mattress in the living room with the TV. On the first day we got there, we didn't do much because Grandma was tired from the ride, and I was a little tired myself. The next day, Aunt Jean took everyone to The Coca-Cola Factory in Atlanta. It was a big place where they made Coca-Cola products, and they had shopping centers and other fun things to do. I had fun walking, shopping, and talking with Jahlil. Surprisingly, he talked a lot, and we just talked about everything. Jahlil and I discussed where we lived; he talked about Atlanta and I told him about Philly. He had never been to Philly before, and I had never been to Atlanta, so we exchanged stories about our neighborhoods and schools. When we got home and settled in, we watched TV together in the living room with Grandma and Aunt Jean until it was time for bed. Aunt Jean and Grandma went into their room, and Jahlil helped me blow up the mattress that I was sleeping on before going into his room for bed. I put on my pajamas and watched TV until I fell asleep. In the middle of the night, Jahlil came into the living room and got into bed with me. I felt the bed topple a little when he got in.

I looked at him and said, "What are you doing in here? You should be sleeping in your room."

"When I can't sleep, sometimes I come in here to watch TV on the couch until I get tired enough to fall asleep," he answered.

"Well, why don't you get on the couch?" I asked, scared and annoyed.

"Or I could just lay with you and keep you company." he responded, putting his arm around my chest, and moving closer to me.

I felt afraid as the flashback of Uncle P flashed through my mind of him smothering me, with his hand around my mouth and his other arm around my body to restrain me. It was like I was playing the same scene from a movie in my head over and over, except I was in the movie. I froze in the moment as he started to touch my nipples and then my vagina through my clothes. In my mind, I thought I could take him; he was only a few years older and a little taller than me, but he was skinny. After that, I thought, *why fight? I'm tired of fighting, just let it happen.*

I let Jahlil touch me inappropriately, and it started to feel good to me. No, I didn't like that he was touching me without my permission, but my body started to respond. I guess my body was going through changes because it felt good. Jahlil took off his pants and got on top of me, poking his penis against my vagina. I still had on my underwear and thin pajama pants. *I can deal with this; he doesn't want to have sex with me; he just wants to play with me;* I thought to myself. *I could just play with him the way I played with Stacey; that's not too bad*, I thought to myself. The feeling made me moan as he continued to hump me until the point of ejaculation. When he was done, he got up and went into his room. I got up and changed my underwear and pajama pants because they were wet and sticky. I returned to my bed and went to sleep. I was happy that we didn't have sex, because although I wasn't a virgin, I wasn't ready to fully give myself away sexually yet on my own.

Jahlil and I continued to "play" with each other for the next few days without anyone knowing what was going on. We continued to talk throughout the day, stealing kisses and touches from each other when we could without Grandma and Aunt Jean noticing. One night, when Grandma and Aunt Jean were sleeping, Jahlil and I were spooning in the living room on the blow-up mattress. Aunt Jean suddenly walked in on us and didn't say a word. I pretended to be asleep, and Jahlil was up watching TV. I was so scared because I thought Aunt Jean was going to say something about Jahlil being behind me, but she didn't say anything. She went into the kitchen to get a snack and went back into her room. I was so confused as to why she thought that our behavior was appropriate. Maybe she thought because we were "Family," we weren't doing anything inappropriate, but we sure were. When she went into the room, we both started quietly laughing. When Jahlil got tired enough, he went back into his room to go to sleep.

When it was time to leave, I was ready to go, but somehow, I didn't want to leave Jahlil. It was the weirdest feeling ever, but I had to go back to Philly. We exchanged numbers and kept in touch for a little while, but then eventually stopped talking, never seeing each other again.

The last strange and scary encounter happened early one fall morning; around 5:30 a.m., I was leaving the house to go to high school. Like most fall mornings, it was dark outside, like it was still nighttime, but it was 5:30 in the morning. It was so dark out that the stars in the morning sky glistened and showed no sign of daybreak. It was my senior year in high school; I had to travel from Mt. Airy, where I lived with Ms. Joanne, and traveled to West Philly every morning, which explained why I left the house so early. This one particular morning, I was walking from my house to the bus stop, which was about two blocks away from the house. After passing a set of large bushes, I noticed a strange sound behind me. It sounded like something was in the bushes, like some type of animal, maybe a cat or something. At first, I didn't think of it as anything; I just knew I heard something. As I continued to walk, I understood the sound clearly; it sounded like flat feet, like someone was walking with no shoes or socks on. I turned around to see what the actual sound was, and about 30 ft away from me was a tall, black, naked man walking behind me. This man had to be about 6 ft tall, and was totally butt naked: not a piece of fabric on him at all. I quickly turned around thinking *what the hell,* and continued to walk, but much faster than before. Now, I am generally a fast walker anyway, so at this point I was jogging. For some reason, I felt like I shouldn't make a big deal out of it by running right away, because I didn't want him to chase me. The next thing I heard were those flat feet sounding like they were running. I turned around again, and as I thought, the naked man was running toward me; and I had to figure out what to do next. Fear ran through my body and caused me to forget about the heavy bookbag I was wearing; it was full of books, clothes, and sports gear, so I just ran for my life. I was about a half a block away and was getting close to the bus stop where I had to cross the street. I was running on the right side of a block where there was nothing but large trees and bushes, with houses at a distance behind them. Across the street, is where the bus stop was, and there were houses facing me. I ran as fast as I could to get across the street, not looking back, just focused on getting to the bus stop, yelling "HELP, SOMEBODY HELP ME!" Once I reached the bus stop, I ran straight to the corner house, banging on the door, ringing the doorbell yelling, "HELP ME PLEASE!" All the while, I was

247

looking behind me to see if I saw the naked man. Across the street, I spotted the naked man hiding behind the tall trees and bushes. Maybe he was waiting to see if someone was going to come out and help me, before deciding if he was going to attack me or continue to chase me.

No one at the house answered, but the next-door neighbor came running out of his house in his police uniform asking, "Are you okay? What is the problem?"

I quickly ran across the lawn to the officer, out of breath saying, "A naked man was chasing me. He is hiding over there in the bushes!" I pointed towards where I saw the man last.

"Stay right here," the officer commanded, as he put his right hand on his right hip, where his holster was securing his gun. The officer walked across the street, taking his gun out of the holster, cocked it, and held it out yelling, "Anybody there? Come out with your hands up!" but no one responded. The officer walked closer to the bushes and didn't see or hear anyone.

"There is no one there," the officer said.

"I know he was there; he was chasing me, and then went into the bushes when I started yelling for help," I explained.

The officer looked at me and said, "We have been getting this complaint lately, so I know you are telling the truth. Where are you on your way to?"

"I'm waiting on the bus so I can go to school," I responded.

"Okay, I will wait for your bus, so I can watch you get on safely," the officer promised.

"Thank you so much officer!" I exclaimed.

My bus arrived within the next five minutes. I got on the bus, still shaking and afraid to go anywhere. I called my Aunt Sandi and told her what was going on. She was so upset about my experience, that she picked me up from school to take me home later that day. She picked me up the next morning, and every morning after to take me to school for the rest of the school year. Aunt Sandi lived in West Philly and worked in North Philly, so she made a huge commitment every day, to travel from West Philly to Mt. Airy, and drove back to West Philly to take me to school, only to travel back to North Philly to go to work. I learned how to be on time that year. If I wasn't ready when she got to my house, early in the morning, she was going to chew me out. When Aunt Sandi pulled up to the house, I had better be dressed and walking out the door. At the time, I didn't notice the sacrifice she made for me in my senior year. Looking back now, I am ever so grateful to have had Aunt Sandi in my corner. This was a time in my life when I didn't think I could be loved, yet I was being loved, and didn't realize it. So, on a personal note, *I love you, Aunt Sandi, and thank you for loving me!*

CHAPTER NINETEEN
AUNT SANDI

I first met Sister Sandrine (Aunt Sandi), at church when Grandma introduced my sisters and me to the church. At first, it was just a general greeting to Aunt Sandi; it wasn't a personal greeting or anything. I met her during the right hand of fellowship, when everyone came up to hug us, after officially joining the church. Aunt Sandi was one church member who came to church for church, and when the church was over, she left immediately. Usually, churchgoers, *and those who are churchgoers know what I'm about to say,* stay after church to socialize with each other. The pastor would give the benediction (the blessing to leave service and go on to live peaceably until we meet again) saying, "May the grace of our Lord and Saviour Jesus Christ and the sweet communion of the Holy Spirit rest, rule, and abide with each of you forever and ever. Amen!" As soon as he finished, first, everyone turned to each other and started to hug and kiss, giving their goodbyes until the next service. Then, people would meet up with other members around the church to talk about the service, how high the spirit (The Holy Spirit) was, and talk about their plans for the week. People usually didn't leave the church for another hour after the service ended, but Aunt Sandi did not go to church to socialize with anyone. She came to church to experience God, so that she could be on her way to navigate through life. Sunday after Sunday for a while, Aunt Sandi left right after church, so I really didn't get the chance to get to know her; however, that changed when she started to participate in church activities and attend church functions.

Aunt Sandi started to attend services regularly, which included Bible study, and any outdoor event offered through the church. The more she attended services, the more I got to know her better. She was down to earth, but just by looking at her, you could tell she didn't play, *it looked like she didn't take no stuff, from anybody.* I knew she didn't play when I saw that she wore dress pants to church. *Come on somebody, y'all know how the church was back in the day; we could not wear pants at church.* Even though our church was not as strict on the dress code, there was this unspoken, traditional rule about pants in the church. There was this one time when an elder in the church, said something to her about wearing dress pants, and instructed her on how she should be wearing skirts and dresses, and Aunt Sandi responded, "Show me in the Bible where Jesus said I can't wear dress pants to church. If you can't find it, then I don't want to hear it." Aunt Sandi was about 5'3" and wore a short boy-cut hairstyle and her pants outfits. She did not care about what people thought about her, inside or outside of the church. If someone had a problem with her, she was going to get to the bottom of it, by any means necessary. It didn't matter whether you were a child or an adult; if she needed to check you, she would. If a child was staring at her, she'd say something like, "Didn't your mama teach you manners, that it's not polite to stare at people? Well, if they didn't, I'mma tell you. It's not polite to stare at people without speaking." If adults were staring at her, she would just come out and ask, "Is there a problem, and if there is, we can step outside," in a calm but ready-to-fight way. Aunt Sandi ruffled a few feathers in the church when she first started attending, because she was a no-nonsense person, *and y'all know it be some nonsense going on in churches*, but she was also very caring and helpful, especially with the youth at the church.

The youth group was big, and Aunt Sandi assisted and chaperoned at almost every youth meeting, which included overnight prayer events, picnics, youth retreats, and youth pow-wows. She had a way with teens that made us feel comfortable connecting with her, without us feeling condemned. The seasoned saints, the (older church people) were judgmental about how we spoke or acted as if they were never children, but Aunt Sandi understood us. They were sometimes judgmental towards the youth, because of the way we dressed, especially about wearing stockings. *I hated wearing stockings; they were so itchy.* There were times when she stood up for some of us, when we were being reprimanded for not wearing stockings. If an elder upset one of the youth by asking, "Where are your stockings? You are a young lady, and should always wear stockings with a skirt," and if word got back to Aunt Sandi, she would step in and respond, "Instead of pressuring these young children about wearing stockings, you should be glad that they are here in church. I don't believe God is worrying about whether they are wearing stockings. Leave the kids alone and talk to their parents if you have something to say." Aunt Sandi didn't correct us too much, unless we were being disrespectful or just doing too much, *which was expected of pubescent teens.* Instead of tearing us down, she told us when we were wrong and encouraged us to do better. She was a strong advocate for the youth, and became especially fond of me, and took me under her wing.

Aunt Sandi and I got closer after I moved out of Sister Martry's house; partially because she was assigned to me by Aunt Aza and partially because she saw that I needed extra emotional, and mental support and she wanted to be there for me. Aunt Aza was good at finding the needs of the youth and meeting those needs with tangible resources, which included using people as resources. One day after a Sunday service, I was waiting at the trolley stop across the street from the church. I was on my way to my new foster home in Mt. Airy when Aunt Sandi saw me and called me back across the street in front of the church.

"Where do you live?" she asked.

"I live in Mt. Airy," I responded.

"Come on, I'll take you home," she said as she signaled for me to follow her to her car.

I responded, "Are you sure? It's kind of far from here."

Aunt Sandi turned and rolled her head towards me, tilting it, and looked at me saying, "If I wasn't willing to take you, I would not have told you to come, so do you want a ride or not?"

"Yes," I answered as I followed her to her car with an attitude in my head.

I was embarrassed because I didn't want to come off as needy, even though I really wanted a ride home, and I was glad because I didn't have to take that long ride home on the bus. It took me about an hour and a half to get home from church on the bus on a Sunday, sometimes longer because of the Sunday bus schedule. Aunt Sandi lived in West Philly at the time. I didn't understand why she would leave West Philly to take me to Mt. Airy and then drive all the way back to West Philly without wanting something in return. During the ride, my mind was going a thousand miles an hour, wondering why she was being so nice to me. We talked a little bit about church and school, but for most of the ride, we were quiet as the radio played.

When we reached my house, she said, "Here, take my number and call me when you need a ride to church. If I'm going to church, I will pick you up and take you home." I was so surprised, because I couldn't believe she would just commit to something like this for me. Although I was still wondering why she was doing it for me, it was something about Aunt Sandi that made me feel comfortable enough to accept her commitment. She read her number aloud, and I saved it into my cell phone. "Thank you so much for dropping me off." I said as I started to get out of the car. From that day on, Aunt Sandi became like a parental figure to me, and she continued to honor her commitment, plus more.

As Aunt Sandi continued to pick me up for church, she and I got more comfortable around each other. On the forty-five-minute ride to church, we didn't talk much; we just let the radio play. Aunt Sandi used to play her gospel music loudly and sing along with one hand on the steering wheel and the other moving up and down on top of the gear shifter to the beat of the music. It was always funny to hear Aunt Sandi sing because she had vibrato in every word she sang, and sometimes she'd even adlib "You're the lifter of my soul

Jesus," no matter what song was playing. On some of the rides to church, we talked and I began to tell her about my family's history and some of the things I was experiencing. There were times I would be so depressed about my life, and she would be there to encourage me through those challenging times. I could call her at any time, no matter what time of night, and she would answer the phone and even come and pick me up and take me to her house for the night. Aunt Sandi lived with her mother, Ms. Cary, who was so nice to me and allowed me to stay at house on weekends. Neither Aunt Sandi nor Ms. Cary were emotional people; they didn't show physical or emotional affection towards each other, but they both cared for me by taking care of me when I was at their house. They lived in a clean, four-bedroom house and gave me my own room to sleep in whenever I stayed the night. Either Ms. Cary or Aunt Sandi would cook breakfast, lunch, and dinner for me, and their food was good, especially Aunt Sandi's French toast! When we were not eating together or out shopping together, we were all in our separate rooms. During my menstrual cycle, I experienced bad cramps, nausea, and headaches. Aunt Sandi would let me lie down in my room while she served me hot tea, Tylenol, and a heating pad. Aunt Sandi was always there for me, and she never left me home alone. In fact, I never saw Aunt Sandi hang out with people, go to the movies, or anything. I never even saw her drink or smoke, and there was no evidence to indicate that she did those things when she was not around me. Aunt Sandi was always home with me; *now, how she spent her time when I was asleep may be a different story,* but the point is that she was present with me and there for me. No one had ever treated me like this before, and I was soaking it all in. Although we didn't hug, kiss, or cry our emotions out, I knew Aunt Sandi cared for me by how she treated and looked after me. I loved being at Aunt Sandi's house because it was quiet. Things went well until we started to annoy each other.

Aunt Sandi and I started to bump heads like in the typical mother and teenage daughter relationship. First, it started when she started buying my clothes; *omg, that was a catastrophe.* We had two totally different kinds of tastes when it came to clothing. She was old-fashioned, not caring about name-brand clothes, but I was the typical teen trying to keep up with the Joneses. I think I was trying to make up for the times when I didn't have nice clothes. I wore hand-me-downs from Goodwill so I wanted to go straight to name-brand clothing. Most of the time, Aunt Sandi took me to JCPenney or Sears to shop for clothes. These were good stores, and they had a variety of clothes, some name brands and some just regular no-name clothes. Of course, Aunt Sandi would pick out something that I didn't like, and I would have to tell her I didn't like what she picked.

One day, she picked out an outfit that I thought looked old for my age, and I said, "I don't like that, it looks old," frowning my face up at the outfit.

"What do you mean old?" she asked as she started to point out all the good things about the outfit. I would then go to pick out something I liked, and she would veto my outfit in some way. We would be frustrated with each other and stop talking to each other, and then we would even leave the store without getting anything. If we weren't battling over clothing, we battled over schoolwork.

Aunt Sandi would get on me about keeping up with my schoolwork. She would make sure I completed my homework at night, and for the most part, I would have already completed it at school. There were times when I had five-page papers due and did not start them until the last minute.

I would ask, "Aunt Sandi, can you help me with this paper I have to write?"

"When is it due?"

"Tomorrow."

"Well, why would you wait until the last minute to start your assignment? How long have you known about this assignment?"

"My teacher gave it to me about two weeks ago," I replied in a scared voice, knowing that I was wrong.

"I'm not helping you. You should've been asked me for help, and you gonna be up all night until you get this paper done!" Aunt Sandi responded, upset.

"Okay, I know I waited until the last minute, but you could still help me. You're just being mean," I exclaimed.

"I ain't mean, but I'm also not doing your work for you. Now shut up and get to work."

Aunt Sandi would be so upset with me for waiting until the last minute, and I would be upset with her because she wouldn't help me. Then we would go to our separate rooms to decompress our frustrations with each other. While I was doing my work, she made me a snack and something to eat to help me stay up and finish my work. It was weird how one minute she was upset with me about something, and the next she was feeding me a snack, but still not helping me. She'd come into my room and say, "Here, this should help you stay up, but you better get this work done tonight," with a smile on her face. I would look at her, so confused as to how the switch-up was so quick. Aunt Sandi would notice the confusion on my face and say, "I ain't mad at you, but you're gonna get this work done." *My confusion did not keep me from enjoying that snack, though.* No matter how much we bumped heads, there was nothing I could do to keep Aunt Sandi from caring for me.

Aunt Sandi and I had so much in common, like we were the same person, but with a 25-year age gap. I'd like to say I was her inner child, and by her caring for me, she was healing herself. She was interesting, but she would do anything for anyone, and most of all, she didn't play about me.

CHAPTER TWENTY
CHURCH HURT

Hurt is hurt, but church hurt is the worst because although humans are flawed, I expected better from the church folk. Many times, you would hear non-churchgoers talking about how churchgoers are hypocrites and how they don't really follow after Christ. As a fellow churchgoer, I understand that no one is exempt from sin, not the leaders of the church, nor the members, so now as an adult, I can understand why certain people have mistreated me; I now know that *no one is perfect,* but as a child I couldn't comprehend the mishandling of my spirit from people in the church. This is not to put any church down because like I said, I understand that humans are flawed, which means no one is perfect. Please understand that the church itself, or every person in the church, was not part of my church hurt. I am simply telling a few memories about a few people who happened to be in the church that also happened to hurt me.

I loved Grandma, and I know that she wouldn't have done anything to hurt me personally, but it was her son who inflicted pain on me. After I was taken away from Grandma (who then became known as Ms. Martry again) because of the rape case I had against her son, she and her family started to treat me differently. My friends who lived across the street from Ms. Martry would call me and ask me what happened. When they called Ms. Martry's house for me, one of her daughters would pick up and say, "That bitch don't live here no more. Stop calling," and hang up the phone. At the time, my friends didn't know what was going on; they didn't know that I had moved out, and they didn't know the reason. They were just calling to check on me to see why I hadn't been outside and coming around to their houses as I did almost daily. When my friends told me this, I was so shocked; for some reason I thought that at least someone would try to ask me my side of the story, but they automatically took their family's side. I continued to attend the same church after that. Ms. Martry introduced me to this church when I first moved into her home. I loved the fellowship, and the worship, and I believed I had become part of the church family. It was in the back of my mind to stop attending this church and find a new one so I didn't have to see Ms. Martry every Sunday, but I had made so many friends and I was involved in almost every ministry, and I loved the way the church supported me throughout the years. Most of all, that was where I found God. I did not want to give up on God because some of his children mistreated me. So, I decided to stay; *I may have also been a little stubborn because I didn't want it to look like I was running away from anything or anyone.* I went to Sunday school, all the services, and still served on the ministries I was a part of, despite the dirty looks I was getting from Ms. Martry. One day I was singing in the choir in the front of the church, and she was to my left in the third pew from the front. I am an alto, so I sang on the right side of the choir facing the right side of the church, *only choir singers know what I'm talking about. The choir was divided by voice ranges; the sopranos stood on the left, tenors in the middle, and altos stood on the right.* Ms. Martry was staring at me, rolling her eyes, and making me feel uncomfortable with her look of disapproval. *Yes, she was doing this in the middle of church, y'all.* I did everything not to look at her, but for some reason, my eyes kept locking on to hers and sometimes we would just stare at each other like I was singing to her personally. All I could do was to continue to sing, try to get my mind off the human staring me down, and focus on Jesus. Sometimes I was successful and sometimes I wasn't. It got so bad that she started to bring people to church with her, and they would also give me dirty looks.

Usually, Ms. Martry came to church by herself; when I was living with her, it was just the two of us and occasionally Stacey, who was her real granddaughter that was about two years younger than me, but now all of a sudden, she would bring visitors. Ms. Martry came to church a few times with her daughter, granddaughter, one of her sons, and one of her best friends, Ms. Cleo. The first time they came together, they all stared at me. Stacey made mad faces and rolled her eyes at me. Her daughter, who attended the church more often than the rest of Ms. Martry's children, gave me a look of disgust. I really wanted to stop going to church that day, because either I was going to flip out on everybody or I was going to have to leave the church. I didn't want to flip out on those people in church because then everyone would be looking at me like I was crazy. If I flipped out, I would have behaved in a way that none of them would have expected; they had known me to behave in a respectful manner. Instead, I just took it on the chin (dealt with it) and kept it moving in life. Until Ms. Cleo showed up one service to embarrass me.

One evening service night after church, I was outside waiting for Aunt Sandi to take me home. Ms. Cleo walked out of the church, walked straight over to me, and grabbed me with the intent of telling me off.

"Listen here, little girl. You are causing trouble for everybody, spreading lies about people that have done nothing but been there for you. You ought to be ashamed of yourself," Ms. Cleo scolded.

Caught off guard, I pulled away from her and broke down crying, "I did not lie, I told the truth!"

"YOU ARE A LIAR! YOU ARE NEVER GONNA BE ANYTHING IN LIFE IF YOU KEEP THIS UP, TAMEENA!" Ms. Cleo screamed while pointing her finger at me.

I was hurt, embarrassed, and confused as to why she felt like now was the time to approach me like this, after church. As people were coming out of the church, Ms. Cleo was ripping me a new one saying, "I don't want you hanging around my son anymore, because I don't want you bringing him down. I don't want him to go down the same road you're going down. Leave him alone!" she warned. Ms. Cleo's son Jonathan and I attended West Philly High together. He was a year or two ahead of me, but we still crossed paths during school and conversed a few times. We also talked outside of school because he was Grandma's godson. Everything was fine between us as friends, although Jonathan was very friendly.

"What, I barely..." I said this before Aunt Sandi came outside and rushed between us.

Someone must have gone inside the church and told my aunt what was going on because she had come out ready to fight. *Everybody has that one aunty who doesn't care where they are at, they will fight whoever, for whatever, wherever, for their nieces and nephews.*

"Shut up, Meena and get in the car," Aunt Sandi ordered.

"But she..." I tried to rebut.

"I said get in the car, Meena," Aunt Sandi warned, and I did what she said. The car was sitting close to where the conversation was taking place, so I could hear some of the things that were being said.

"First of all, that is a child; if you have anything to say to her you go to her adult, which is me. I'm not gonna sit up here and let you talk down to my child like that. If you have something to say, say it to me, but I guarantee you it's not gonna go well," Aunt Sandi threatened.

"You better be careful because she is going to lie on you too," Ms. Cleo said.

"You better just get going before I do something in front of the house of God that I'm going to have to repent for later," Aunt Sandi said, motioning her hand for Ms. Cleo to go away.

Honestly, I forgot my aunt was inside because I was prepared to handle this on my own. That's the way I was used to doing things, on my own, but God had placed people in my life like Aunt Sandi to ride for me (support me) when I needed help. Ms. Cleo left because she didn't want that smoke (she didn't want to get beat up). Aunt Sandi got in the car and drove off as we talked about what happened on the ride home. I was so grateful for Aunt Sandi stepping in like that for me, but I was still so hurt by the things Ms. Cleo said to me. She made me feel like I was this troubled child who wasn't going to be successful in life. I was down for a little bit after that altercation, but I sucked it up because I was already dealing with another situation at the church. That one, no one knew about, still until this day, well, until they crack this book open.

There was an older guy at church that was so nice and helpful, but he couldn't keep his hands to himself nor off my body. At the age of 15, I was hanging out with a group of friends that attended the church. We would go out to the movies, bowling, game nights, and each other's houses. One of the siblings in the group had an older brother who acted as our chaperone most of the time. He would take us wherever we went and would drop us off back home. This chaperone was in his late 20s at the time, and he was very kind to everyone in our group; he was especially kind to me. When we went out to eat as a group, he would sit across from me at the table all the time and he would pay for my meal. He would ask me if I was alright a few times a night, often rubbing my hands, or my shoulders, or giving me a hug. It was so weird at first, but I just thought he liked me. I never played into it because I wasn't physically attracted to him, but he never gave up pursuing me.

One night after an outing, he dropped everyone off at home, and he dropped me off at home last. I have to add that he had a sister that went with us everywhere, and he would drop her off before dropping everyone else off, which I thought was backward.

I asked him one time, "Why don't you drop everyone else off first and then go home with your sister?"

He answered, "Because I am going out after this; I'm not going straight home." It still didn't make sense to me, but he was the driver. This particular night after dropping everyone off, he left me for last; as we were getting closer to my house, he pulled the car to the side. Without saying anything, he turned the car off, turned his body towards me on the passenger side, and started kissing me on my lips. Shocked, I just sat there with my mouth closed before putting my hand out to push him back.

"I'm sorry, I thought you liked me. I see the way you look at me when we're out together," he said as he started to rub his hand on and between my legs.

"I don't look at you like anything, and I don't want you touching me like this," I said with an attitude, but he did not listen. He climbed over to my side as I tried to pull the lock up to unlock the door and get out of the car, but he pushed the lock down as he got on top of me. He was a heavy guy; he laid his torso on me while trying to use his hands to take off my pants. "STOP, STOP" I yelled, but he didn't listen, and he didn't respond. I continued to try to push him off of me, then I finally gave up. He was too strong, and I was afraid he would hit me. He did his "business" and then took me home; he drove the rest of the way home in silence like nothing ever happened. Once again, I was betrayed and had to deal with it by myself because I knew no one would believe me. They would think it was consensual because of the way he acted towards me whenever we met, and I didn't want to disappoint his family. I suffered in silence, as I saw this guy every Sunday pretend that he didn't rape me, and as we continued to go on our usual outings with the group.

That hurt me a lot, but what hurt me the most was when I later found out in life that, before me, this person was accused of molesting a child in church. It hurt to find out that he was kicked out of the church and then allowed back when he got older. I wondered why no one told me to watch out for this person, not hang around this person, and why this person was still allowed to hang around minors. I guess the group I was with didn't know, but his parents and the parents of that child knew. I felt betrayed by the church — the whole group — but I kept the secret of my assault buried inside of me because I never wanted to be looked at like the girl who was always accusing people of molesting and raping her, and I never wanted to potentially lose all my friends. I've been hurt by many strangers before, but being hurt by people you know who go to church, made me feel unsafe and unworthy.

CHAPTER TWENTY-ONE
OFF TO COLLEGE

It was August 25, 2002, when Aunt Sandi dropped me off at Lincoln University. I was 17 years old and turning 18 in October; I remember feeling excited yet nervous. I was excited because this was my chance to get away from all the nonsense life had thrown at me, from moving from foster home to foster home, and all the other stuff in between. While college would provide another place for me to live after getting kicked out of Ms. Joanne's house, it would be my first place without a legal guardian to oversee or mishandle me. That thought made me nervous because I knew I was on my own and responsible for myself. How could something I had longed for so deeply and for so long, make me feel so inadequate and unprepared? Perhaps it was exactly what I needed, an outlet for me to make sense of my new world, a world of trying to forget the pain of the past. I believed it was definitely part of God's plan for my life.

A few nights before I left to go to college, my church threw me a surprise going-away party at the church. *They got me, y'all.* I had absolutely no idea that this was going on behind my back. It was a Sunday afternoon, right after morning service, and Tattiana, Jinniyah, and I went to the store after church, as we often did on Sundays. In fact, it had become so routine that they made it part of the plan to keep me away from the church for a few minutes while everyone set up. We went to the store, chatted outside the church for a little bit, and then we went inside, just as we usually did, to wait around for "the next service." Jinniyah said, "Let's go upstairs and chill," and Tattiana agreed. We all began to walk towards the back of the church to go upstairs. Leading the way was Jinniyah, with Tattiana and then myself following them up the stairs. When I reached the top of the steps, I was startled by a loud "SURPRISE!!" from many people who attended the church. "Oh, my goodness, thank you so much!! Wait, what is all this for?" All I saw were people, food, and unopened gifts. It wasn't my birthday; I graduated from high school two months ago, and I couldn't understand why I was being surprised and celebrated. "We wanted to surprise you with some things you would need for college, so we threw this party for you," Tattiana responded. I just smiled, and a few tears fell from my eyes because, honestly, I had never had a party planned for me before. All my favorite people were there; Aunt Sandi, Aunt Aza, Yani, Jinniyah, Tattitana, and so many more who continued to play an important part in my healing journey. It touched my heart so much that people could care for someone they are not related to in such a way. I walked around and gave everyone hugs, expressing my gratitude for their presence *and the presents*. There were gifts, food, games, and just plain old good fun.

I left the party with everything I needed for the first year to make it through college: clothes, sheets, a little hot pot to cook noodles in, lamps, school supplies, toiletries, towels, wash clothes, and so much more. The most surprising gift I received that day was a lavender silk lingerie that reached the top of my thighs. It was surprising because it came from a woman minister who seemed to be very spiritual. The minister said, "Every young lady needs to feel comfortable and beautiful, even when they sleep sometimes. Just promise me that you'll always be alone when you wear this to bed. NO BOYS should be in your dorm room!!" I was still so shocked, but I made the promise, *a promise I didn't keep by the way. Don't judge me; love me, that outfit was cute. I had to show somebody.* This party made me feel special, a feeling I had never felt before. For once, I didn't feel like people were helping me just to take advantage of me; it was because they saw a need, and truly cared, and wanted me to be prepared for college. God has a way of placing people in your life for reasons and seasons, *at least that's what I believed helped me along my life.* Placing me in that church through my first foster home was the best thing that came out of my being in foster care and in my life. I always say that the church raised me because of the different families in the church that played such an important role in my life during my foster care years and beyond. This was another milestone that I didn't have to miss because they had my back by sending me off to college with pride.

On the day I left to go to college, Aunt Sandi picked me up from Tattiana's house, packed her car, and drove me to Lincoln University for the first day of school. It was about an hour and a few minutes ride, and Aunt Sandi and I chatted during the ride, and she shared some advice about college safety, staying on top of my studies, and even added a playful "no boys' ' warning. I couldn't help but wonder why everyone seemed so insistent about me not being around boys, but I agreed to heed her advice.

"Why can't I talk to boys anyway? Boys are going to be there, you know," I questioned.

"Because you need to stay focused on your work. There will be time for boys later," Aunt Sandi responded.

"Alright, I guess I'll just stick to talking to girls then!" I joked.

"Stop playing, girl, you know what I mean!" Aunt Sandi replied with a laugh.

We talked and laughed the rest of the ride to Lincoln when I met up with Yani and her family.

We talked about my roommate and what she might be like.

"I hope she's clean," I mentioned.

"Well, if she isn't, you just keep your side clean, and have a conversation with her if it's too much for you." Aunt Sandi responded.

"By the way, why didn't you and Yani become roommates?" Aunt Sandi asked.

"Well, we decided we wanted to make new friends, and we didn't want to risk our friendship by living together," I responded. Yani and I talked about the pros and the cons of being roommates when we applied for college. Some pros were that we would live together and hang around each other all the time. We didn't know if we wanted to get used to living with a stranger and the possibility of not getting along with that stranger. Some cons would be that we lived together and then noticed some things about each other that we didn't know and disliked. We didn't want to get tired of each other and risk our friendship ending for the rest of our lives. That last con was what really drove our decision to have different roommates and I believe it was the best decision we made, because we are still Besties to this day. We did what we said and we made new friends and kept our friendship intact.

I had gotten my room assignment and roommate's information in the mail a few weeks prior, so I was trying to feel her out by the way her name looked on the paper. *Oh, don't judge me, y'all. Y'all know names mean stuff and most people act the way their name sounds.* My roommate's name was Valencia Valdez, so I assumed she was Hispanic, light-skinned, with long hair to the middle of her back. Aunt Sandi told me not to judge a book by its cover, or in this case, a person by their name.

Yani and I reached Lincoln around the same time, and we made sure we stayed together while registering for everything. She got dropped off by her mother and sisters. Aunt Sandi helped me set up my room, and Yani's mom and sisters helped her set up her room. It was a cool process because Yani and I kept going back and forth between rooms, seeing the progress we each made, and Aunt Sandi and Yani's mom did, too. We were so excited to see each other, and we *were hype* to meet our roommates.

We had to pay $5.00 for our room key, and I didn't have the money, so I asked Aunt Sandi for the money. I had already annoyed Aunt Sandi because when she picked me up from Jinnyiah's house, I had my clothes in trash bags, and all my gifts were in the same gift bags from when I received them. Aunt Sandi had brought me suitcases, but they kind of got ruined in the hustle and bustle of me moving from house to house. On top of that, I had worked all summer and didn't have money to pay for my room key.

"Aunt Sandy, can I have five dollars so I can get my room key?"

"How is it that you worked all summer and you don't have five dollars for your key?"

"I didn't know I had to pay for the key." I responded with an attitude.

"So, you mean to tell me you couldn't save any money this summer, so you could have what you needed for school?" she scolded.

At the time, I didn't think of it as a big deal, but looking back as an adult now, I see where Aunt Sandi was coming from. I should have at least had that because I did have a job working at the Dollar Tree. Yani's mom took care of everything for Yani, so I guess I was looking at her family's dynamics and assumed mine would be the same. Anyway, Aunt Sandy did give me the $5.00 so I could get my room key. I realized that I had to be a little bit more responsible for myself. It wasn't like I couldn't depend on anyone because I was able to depend on Aunt Sandi, but here I was alone with not even $5.00 to pay for a room key, a key that I would have to take care of for the rest of the school year. The feeling I felt having to ask for money from someone who wasn't my family by blood made me feel alone, embarrassed, and needy. This wasn't a great way to start out my freshman year at college; not only did that experience make me feel bad about myself, it pushed me to do things for myself and to want more for and from myself. I was encouraged to do my best so that I would never have to ask anyone for anything ever again. Aunt Sandi helped me set up my room, and then left. I became an independent college student, excited to start my freshman year of college.

CHAPTER TWENTY-TWO
FRESHMAN WEEK

The anticipation of starting college as a freshman gave me a profound sense of independence I never knew could exist. I had to juggle my own entertainment, social life, and education. Fortunately, having Yani there by my side made it easier for me to open up.

During this week, which was exclusively for first-year students, Yani and I went on a mission to make friends. While we waited for our roommates to arrive, we introduced ourselves to the other students on our dorm floor. We didn't want to seem desperate by walking into someone's room and saying, "Hi, I'm Meena; what's your name?" That seemed a bit awkward, so to break the ice, we decided to explore different rooms and compliment the students on how well they had decorated their spaces. I didn't realize people took decorating their dorm rooms so seriously. As we entered each room, there were color schemes, themes, and decor, which made it easier to spark conversations with our fellow freshmen. Some people gave us strange looks for our enthusiasm, which made me ready to quit *because I have my best friend already. I'm okay if I don't make another friend,* I thought, but some of them still cautiously introduced themselves.

As we stepped into a room, a burst of vibrant purple hues immediately caught our attention. Yani's face lit up — purple was her favorite color, and the room seemed tailor-made for her. While I didn't have a particular favorite color, the different shades of purple appealed to me instantly.

"Wow, this is nice. Purple is my favorite color! I'mma call this the Purple Room! I'm Yani, and this is my best friend, Meena," Yani explained.

"Yes, to the Purple! We were just going around meeting our floormates. Your room looks really good," I added.

The roommates were thankful and proud of their work as they explained they had planned their decor with shades of lavender and violet over the summer. There were beds on either side of the room. One bed had lavender pillows with a violet comforter, and the other bed had the opposite, violet pillows with a lavender comforter. Both roommates had a string of purple lights over their beds with pictures of themselves on their respective sides with friends and family members hung on the cream covered walls. On the floor were lavender and violet plush rugs, right in front of each bed. The room had a great vibe; I wasn't even worried about introductions because I was enjoying the scenery of their room. It made me think of what my room could have looked like if I had used a color scheme. *If I only knew, I could have made my side of the room more interesting,* I thought. I was totally grateful for my church throwing me that surprise going away party. I just never thought I could make my dorm room a home. So far, I was 0/4 in making houses my home. *Although, I don't have a favorite color, I don't have family pictures to put on my wall, no posters of famous people that I fanned, no money, and no one to give me money, so...*, I finished my thought with just being grateful for what I had. We continued to enter rooms, alternating between being the first to introduce ourselves. The process was both fun and rewarding, as we made new friends on the first day of college.

Yani and I met three friends from two rooms. From the first room, we met Daneka and Judith; Daneka was from Philly and

Judith was from the Virgin Islands, and they got along well. In the second room, we met Clarrissa and Marilyn. Clarrissa was also from Philly and Marilyn was also, surprisingly, from the Virgin Islands. In this room, we noticed that Judtih and Marilyn looked exactly alike. They both were light-skinned, with reddish colored hair, the same height, and thick boned. It turned out that Judith and Marilyn were identical twins. I thought it was cool that the twins decided to live in separate rooms instead of rooming together. I asked why they decided to separate, and they both said, "We've been together our whole lives," at the same time; it was so funny. They were kind of in the same situation as Yani and me; they wanted to room independently to make new friends. While we were all talking and introducing ourselves, Clarrissa sat on her bed, engrossed on her laptop. She didn't look up at us, nor did she contribute to the conversation. During our conversation, we decided to leave the room and see if we could meet new friends.

"Clarrissa, you want to go walk around with us?" Marilyn asked.

Clarrissa responded, "No, thank you," with a half-smile.

Daneka, Judith, Marilyn, Yani, and I left to walk the halls of our dorm, hoping to make new friends. The excitement of Yani and I meeting our roommates lingered in the back of our minds, so we walked to Yani's room first, and there sat her roommate on her bed.

Yani was the first one to enter her room when I heard a "Heyyyyy girl!" from her roommate Chauna. I stepped back, and my head cocked to the side because she was acting like they had known each other for a long time. They did talk and meet over the phone when they got their roommate assignments, but Chauna was hype like they were best friends. She was so energetic, she jumped off her bed and hugged Yani. Yani jumped back in surprise, but then matched her energy, saying, "Oh, heyyyy girl!" hugging her back. As I glanced at Chauna's side of the room, I saw that she had purple bedding, and posters of different boy groups on her wall. *Ugh, purple must be her favorite color, too,* I thought, rolling my eyes. Instantly, I thought Chauna was trying to steal my best friend. They talked on the phone a few times during the summer and learned that both of their favorite colors are purple, and they were hype. *I'm gonna have to fight this girl for my best friend, ain't I? I have been doing good not getting into trouble, but I'm not fittna let this girl steal my best friend,* I thought until Yani introduced us.

"Chauna, this is my best friend, Meena," Yani introduced. If I knew Yani, she probably was thinking like, *gurl you hype!* I thought to myself, *yes that's my best friend, so you can relax a lot!* To know that Yani claimed me as her best friend set the record straight for Chauna and everyone in the room. It also made me feel confident in our relationship, a feeling I had never felt with anyone else before this point. Friends have come and gone, but Yani and I have remained the same for the past 7-8 years. They needed to know that we would be best friends forever and that nothing could come between us. I needed them to know that no matter how friendly we are to them, they won't ever come close to the friendship Yani and I had developed.

"HEYYY, GIRRL!" I answered, hugging Chauna sarcastically.

"Heyy, Meena! That's so cool that you guys are best friends and at the same college!" She replied with the same energy she gave Yani.

I was pleased to know that she was naturally energetic, because I was ready to go in on this girl.

Yani started to introduce all our new friends to Chauna, and she continued to be energetic with everyone. She was a little extra with it, but at least she wasn't emotionless like Clarrissa. Chauna made it known that she was ready to go visit the boys' dorms. By looking at the posters on her wall of B2K, 112, and the Backstreet Boys, all of which had opened shirts or no shirts on at all, I could tell she was boy crazy. Yani laughed saying, "Girl, slow down, you just got here. The rest of us ain't thinking 'bout no boys yet." We all looked at each other, laughing, and agreeing with Yani, but also acknowledging the key word "YET" as we laughed and emphasized "YET" simultaneously. Chauna went her way to start her boy expedition, and we went our way to see if my roommate was in my room.

I was the first to enter my room, and I saw Valeria finishing up her side. Her back was to the door, and she was tucking the final corner of her bed in. Everyone was waiting in the hallway, as I waited until she finished tucking her bed in to introduce myself. She turned around and jumped, putting her hand across her chest, when she saw me and the squad with me.

"Ooo, you scared me!" she said slowly.

"Hi, I'm Meena; I'm your roommate. My bad, I didn't mean to scare you," I responded as I waved my hand.

"I'm Valeria," she pronounced slowly and properly.

Oh wow, she is going to be annoying with her proper, slow voice, I thought to myself. She spoke properly, but her voice lingered with each word she spoke. It was so slow and monotone, showing no expression. Even when she laughed, it was slow, showing the bare minimum of expression. If this was her personality, then I guess I would have to accept it. Valeria was brown-skinned, about 5'6" with dark hair to her shoulders. I definitely judged her by her name, and was all wrong. I didn't know where she was from because of her accent, so I said, "I'm from Philly!" trying to get her to tell me where she was from without asking.

"Oh, I'm from Barbados, but I live in Jersey now," Valeria responded.

Don't judge me, y'all, but at the time I did not know anything about Barbados; I had never heard of it, but I pretended to.

"Cool, how is it there?" I asked, trying to get a feel of where Barbados was on the map.

"It's nice; I love it. It's a small island with beautiful beaches and stuff," she responded.

I could tell she was getting annoyed with me asking all my questions; *truth be told, I was tired of asking her questions. She seemed so uppity. I wasn't a fan,* so I just stopped and waited for her to ask me questions, but she didn't. Yani and our new friends walked into my room, and I introduced them to Valeria.

"Wow, you met friends already," Valeria said sarcastically.

"Yeah, we were waiting for you to come," I mentioned matter of factly.

"Welp, I'm here now," she laughed slowly with a sarcastic tone.

I really don't like your sarcasm. I can fix that for you, I thought to myself.

Other than her slow speaking and sarcasm, it turned out Valeria fit right in with us; although she was the prissy one of the group, we all hung together all freshman week and beyond.

Freshman week was so much fun. It was filled with different activities, "motivational" gatherings, and trips. The upperclassmen led us around campus to show us the different dorms and buildings while giving us historical information about the college. Some of it was motivational like, "Don't be afraid if this is your first time away from home," "do your best," "college is the place for you to find yourself because you can fit in anywhere." Blah blah blah. Then the motivational speech took a turn for the worst when our guide said, "Look to the person to your left and to the person to your right; there is a chance that you won't see that person by graduation." *Wow, that just went south quickly,* I thought to myself. The leaders gave statistics that many students who start college do not graduate on time or at all. Then the one that got me was according to statistics, college students are more likely to carry STDs on campus. *It just doesn't stop,* I said to myself. I get the big picture of protecting yourself and having safe sex, but *dang,* that kept me abstinent for like three months, … *y'all really need to stop judging me.* Other than those downers, freshman week was upbeat; we had game nights, dances, and we ended with a freshman trip to Six Flags.

Our freshman trip to Six Flags was amazing! All six of us boarded the bus and sat in the back together. We talked the whole ride, talking about what rides we were going to get on. I told Yani and the crew that I didn't ride rides because I was too scared of heights, and I just didn't like rollercoasters.

"Oh, you're gonna get on some rides with us; You have to!" Yani demanded.

Valeria chimed in, "You — scared of heights? Wow!" sarcastically.

"Yes, I am, and I'm not ashamed to say it!" I responded, laughing.

We all continued to talk until we reached Six Flags.

When we got there, we got off the bus and the six of us headed for rides and games. Everything I said went right out the window about how I wasn't going to get on rides and stuff. Yani and everyone else talked me into getting on almost all the rides, and I was scared for my life with each one. When one ride we got on started, I didn't like the feeling of my stomach rising to my chest when we dropped from 100 ft in the air in 4.5 seconds. Some of the rides weren't as bad as I thought they would be, even though the initial fear of heights and roller coasters still set in. The girls were cheering me on for every ride and praising me after each ride. I must admit, for me to be so afraid, I had fun and was glad I got on rides with my friends. We played games, did water rides, ate and had so much fun at Six Flags until the last minute before we had to get back on the bus. Everyone was so tired and drained from all the walking, the water, the screaming, but we still made time to talk about how much fun we had on the ride back to campus. Of course, I was the topic of discussion for most of the conversation because they talked about how "scary" I was, but also how proud they were that I participated even when I was scared. It was such a pivotal moment for me because for the first time "on my own," I felt accepted by my peers. I didn't feel like I had to fake conversations, and I could be me and not feel like I had to be like everyone else in my group. True friendships were being made during that trip so much so that by the time we reached campus, all six of our periods came on. Talk about bonding; while we were on our way to school, everyone started complaining about stomach pain and cramps. We took turns going to the bathroom at the back of the bus, and everyone came back with the same news, that our periods were on. Between the six of us we were able to conjure up some pads and tampons to hold us until we got back to campus. There on that bus we declared that we were meant to be friends during our freshman year. The declaration came to fruition from freshman year and beyond.

CHAPTER TWENTY-THREE
COURT DAY

I knew the day would come when I would get the dreaded phone call about the actual date of my court hearing with Uncle P. A representative from the attorney's office called me and informed me that I was to appear in court in two weeks to testify against Uncle P. The formal paperwork was going to be sent directly to me with the exact time and date of the hearing. Now under normal circumstances, I would have been excited to get mail at Lincoln, but this piece of mail killed my excitement about receiving anything at college. It was the first piece of mail I was to receive at college, and I was dreading it. All of a sudden, I would rather be invisible and not thought of again. The phone call was breathtaking, but not in a good or beautiful way. It felt like the oxygen was taken out of my dorm room, and my stomach started to turn and roll in my body. After getting off the phone, my legs turned to jelly as I fell onto my bed, struggling to breathe. My lungs began to tighten as I grabbed my neck, trying to swallow any bit of air I could. "I can't do this, I can't do this, I can't do this," I panted as tears silently began to fall from my eyes. Alone, without a roommate to witness or assist with this embarrassing panic attack, I soon calmly whispered, "I can do this; I have to do this; I don't want him to do this to any more girls. Tameena, you have to do this," I said, encouraging myself.

I was able to regulate my breathing and calm down enough to call my Aunt Aza. I knew she would be able to help me process what I was presently going through and to unpack what I was about to experience in two weeks. The phone rang several times before Aunt Aza finally answered, and with each passing ring, my anxiety grew, afraid she wouldn't respond.

"Aunt Aza, I don't know what to do or what to say in court. No one is going to believe me because I am a foster child," I cried in fear.

"Tameena, Tameena, take a deep breath. Listen to me. You know exactly what to do; you tell the truth. Your part is to show up and tell the truth, and let God handle the rest, baby," Aunt Aza replied.

"I don't want to see him again, Aunt Aza," I sobbed.

"Baby, you must, and it might not feel good, but it will be alright. Think about all of the other little girls he may have hurt and the ones he might try to hurt in the future! You're doing your part, and God will be with you in that courtroom, and so will I," Aunt Aza explained.

She prayed for me on the phone. Although I was anxious, Aunt Aza's prayer brought me comfort.

After my conversation with Aunt Aza, I shifted into survival mode, with little time to build my confidence before testifying against Uncle P and facing Grandma in court. I was engulfed with an array of feelings. I sat in the corner with my arms wrapped around my knees, fists balled, body shaking, worried about how the case was going to end. Thoughts of what people would think of me, to moments of not caring at all flooded my mind. At times, I would reassure myself by saying, "It's gonna be what it's gonna be." I was just ready for the trial to be over with so I could go back to living my life without Uncle P lingering in the back of my head. Little did I know he would always be there, at times taunting me.

Of course, those two weeks flew by like Winter Break to a school teacher. It seemed like I got the phone call, went to sleep, and woke up in the courtroom. That day, I entered the courtroom and was immediately overwhelmed by the adult presence that filled the room. As I opened the doors to the courtroom, I saw an aisle that stretched about 30 feet long and 6 feet wide, which led from the doors to the front of the courtroom. It looked like the aisle of doom. On the right of the aisle were rows of pews where I saw Uncle P's family sitting. There sat Grandma, Aunt B, uncle P's wife, Aunt Vinice, and his daughters, Jordyn and Jody, giving me dirty looks as I passed by. On the left of the aisle sat Aunt Aza and Aunt Sandi, who were there for moral support for me. At the bottom of the aisle, there was a wooden divider separating the spectators from the jury, the lawyers, the security guard, and the judge. On the other side of the divider were two tables, one on the right and one on the left. On the left sat a lawyer and an empty chair that I would fill, and on the right sat a lawyer and Uncle P in his prison uniform with a kufi on his head sitting at a table. It baffles me when criminals go to jail and become spiritual suddenly. *That may have come out wrong the way*

I just mentioned that, but really, why? Now don't get me wrong, everyone should find solace in a religion that fits their personal morals as a human being, but this man's mother was a church-going woman. He very well could have found spirituality before he raped my sisters and me by going to church with his mother and finding Jesus. *So, that still came out wrong, so…. what I meant to say is that "I hope he lives a better life now?"*

Walking into the courtroom filled with adults made me scared and nervous. Despite being four years free from my mother's reins, the courtroom transported me back to the "children ought to be seen and not heard" era, as I was the only child in the courtroom. There were about twelve adults that sat in chairs behind a separate divider, waiting to judge me, *at least that's how I felt at the time*. In the front of the room was a long platform that sat a little higher than everyone else in the courtroom; that was where the judge would sit, guarded by two security guards who stood on either side in front of the judge's stand. I was so worried about what was about to happen. One of the biggest mistakes I made was to take a glance around the room to see what seemed like everyone there was against me. Grandma's face struck me with immediate fear and sadness. I knew I wasn't wrong; I sensed that Grandma was hurt (in denial) by my truth, which she believed to be a lie. A look of anger and disappointment followed me as she stared me down to my seat. Uncomfortably, I sat waiting for the judge to come in and start the session.

When it was time for me to explain what happened, it was very difficult and terrifying. It was too painful to remember what happened to me four years ago, let alone too painful to conjure up that dreadful night and speak about it. I was the first to take the stand, as I was sworn in by taking an oath of truth, saying, "I promise to tell the truth, the whole truth and nothing but the truth, so help me God." The lawyer who represented me asked, "Tameena, can you point to the person who raped you in this courtroom?" Answering his question, I pointed to Uncle P who was sitting in front of me on the left side of the room.

"Tameena, where did this happen?" my lawyer asked.

"This happened in my grandma's house." I responded.

"For the record Tameena, this isn't your real grandma, right?" my lawyer asked.

"No, she was my foster parent at the time," I answered.

"I know this is hard for you, but can you walk me through what happened?" he asked.

"Well, I was sleeping in my bed in the middle of the night. I felt pain between my legs, and when I woke up, Uncle P was behind me." I responded.

"Tameena, when you say you felt pain between your legs, what do you mean? Can you tell the exact place on your body?" my lawyer asked for clarity.

"It was my private area, like my vagina." I answered timidly, fidgeting with my fingers. It was so uncomfortable talking to a man about this incident. I was so embarrassed.

"Okay, so you felt the pain, woke up, and noticed Uncle P behind you, correct?" he clarified.

"Yes."

"And what was he doing behind you?"

"I think he was trying to push his penis inside of my vagina." I stuttered.

"Did you try to move or tell him to stop?"

"I tried, but he was holding my body tight to him and my mouth, so I couldn't say anything. I tried to scream, because it hurt, but he just told me to stop or he was going to kill my sisters." I explained with tears rolling down my eyes.

"That's all for now, Tameena," the lawyer explained.

I sat there on the stand with my head down in fear. While I was talking, I could see Grandma and her crew shaking their heads at me like I was saying something wrong. I was so glad to be finished with those questions because they were uncomfortable. Little did I know the harder questions were going to be followed by Uncle P's lawyer.

Uncle P's lawyer was an older woman, maybe in her forties, who was dressed in a nice gray pants suit. I thought because we both were females, she would show sympathy, but I was sadly mistaken. She looked like she was nice, not realizing she was there to tear me down with her questions. This was before I knew about cross examination in the courtroom.

"Hi, Tameena, how are you feeling today?" she asked. I thought that was a stupid question; *how do you think I'm feeling today? I* wanted to answer.

"Okay, I guess." I lied.

"Tameena, does your Uncle P live in the house with your grandma?"

"No, he doesn't."

"Well, how did he get in the house so late at night?"

"I guess he has a key to his mother's house," I answered.

"So, you're not sure if he has a key or not, but you know he was in the house?" she asked.

"I don't know, but there is no other way he could've gotten into the house without a key," I explained.

I felt like my lawyer should have objected because I didn't see why it mattered that he had a key or not to his mother's house. He was in the house in the middle of the night, which meant he had a key. Most children have a key to their parents' house, even if they don't live with them anymore. At this point, I was irked, and she just kept coming for me.

"Tameena, you said that he came into your room in the middle of the night while you were asleep, correct? she asked.

"Yes."

"So, it's safe to say that it was dark in your room, which would impair your ability to see who exactly was in your room. Especially if he was behind you, like you say. Did you ever get a chance to turn around to see my client's face?" she scolded.

"It was dark, and I didn't see his face, but I knew the sound of his voice when he threatened me; it was him." I explained.

"So, this man raped you, and you didn't see his face, but you know it was him. Did you get to look at him when he left the room?" she asked.

"No, well. kind of. When he got out of my bed, I was too afraid to turn around right away, but I managed to turn a little, and I saw him fastening his belt or something. His back was turned to me, but I saw his body build. He was short and thick, just like him; It was him." I expressed.

"Tameena, but we just can't be sure it was him," she explained.

I was so upset because it seemed like nothing I said was coming out right. Maybe I struggled to articulate my thoughts clearly because when I actually played it back in my head I thought, *well damn, it really doesn't make sense that I didn't see his face, but I am accusing him,* but I know it was him. I started to second guess myself, asking myself if I had accused the wrong man. At the moment, I spent so much time second guessing myself that I didn't have a chance to think about everything else I knew to be true. What I didn't get the chance to explain were all the other times he came into the house while Grandma was in the house to touch me inappropriately, or the times I rode in his car when he touched me inappropriately, or even the time when he raped me at his house. I know this man, and he knows me inside and out, but just when I thought it was over, it got worse.

As I testified, I could see the facial expressions of the jury and Grandma in disbelief. It was as if there was a sign on my face labeled "Lying foster child screaming for attention" on my face. I felt like I was being judged behind the stereotypes of teenage foster children. *You know the statistics that say foster children are bad and that we are either gonna wind up in prison, homeless, or dead.* My lawyer may have objected twice throughout this case. I really think I could've represented myself if I had planned too, but I can't cry over spilled milk. Uncle P's lawyer brought up the fact that I was in foster care and paired it with my diaries that magically showed up in court. She walked over to get my journals and asked, "Tameena, do you know what I have here?" as she swings my three composition books side to side in her hand.

"Yes, those are my journals," I expressed with confusion about how she got ahold of my journals. *Ugh, I left them at Grandma's house,* I remembered. The lawyer chose one journal; there were sticky notes hanging out of the journal on several pages, notes that I did not put there. Those notes were placed as markers for the lawyer to read out to the court. She walked over to my stand and read aloud, "I hate it here. I don't want to live here anymore," then she asked me,

"Tameena, is this the reason why we are all here today, because you didn't want to live with Ms. Martry anymore?"

"What — no," I answered confusedly and with an attitude.

"I want to run away, but I don't have anywhere to go," she read from another entry.

Without me being able to get a word in, she continued to read different entries that only described my responses to the anteceding feelings of my experiences of discomfort from being molested and raped. Y'all, this lawyer used my journals against me to say I always wanted to leave, so I made up a lie that I was raped to get out. It was insane how, out of everything that was written in those journals, she would pick such vague sentences to use against me to help them win the case. I wrote about that night and the other times in my journals with dates that expressed what I was going through at the house, but of course, let's just skip all that other important information. The whole time, Uncle P was sitting there with this stupid smirk on his face, like he knew he was going to win and was ready to be back on the streets.

It was time for the jury to deliberate to come up with a verdict. During the jury's deliberation, I went to the bathroom just to get a different scenery. I went into a stall and sat on the toilet with all my clothes on to cry. In the courtroom, I couldn't show all of my emotions because I had to be strong for myself in front of everyone, but in that stall, I let loose. Silent tears started to fall from my eyes, followed by soft sobbing, snot, and stuff. It only took a few minutes to release the anguish I was feeling in my gut before I left the stall to wash my face and hands. As I walked to the sink to wash my hands, someone came out of the other stall. It was Uncle P's daughter, Jordyn. I caught a quick glimpse of her and quickly turned my head. She stood there, staring me down, like she was thinking of what to do or say. My mind was racing because I was fittna be ready for whatever. At this point, I had nothing to lose, but she said nothing and quickly left the bathroom. For a quick second, I thought she looked like she was on my side, like she knew it happened but couldn't go against her father. Jordyn and I used to be close, and it hurt me to see it all go away so swiftly. I left the bathroom about a minute after her to collect myself before I returned to the courtroom.

The jury returned from deliberation and came to a verdict. One of the officers asked for me and Uncle P to stand where we were at our tables with our lawyers. My heart was pounding a million beats a minute.

"Has the jury reached a verdict?" the judge asked.

The foreperson rose and answered, "Yes, your Honor."
As she reached for the paper and unfolded it, I put my head down, and my heartbeat dropped to its normal pace. I felt a sense of peace that came over my spirit.

"On the account of rape, we find the defendant, Not Guilty," the foreperson announced.
And just like that, the jury was convinced that I was the troubled foster child who would do anything to get my way. I felt like a failure, and for a moment, I felt like I was living up to the statistics society set for me as a foster child. Meanwhile, cheers filled the courtroom from Uncle P's family, happy that he wasn't going back to jail. The peace that fell over me prepared me for the verdict ahead of time. I was able to walk over to Aunt Aza to receive her hugs and a prayer. *Yes, we prayed right in that courtroom.* Aunt Aza would pray anywhere on the spot, and it was just what I needed to make it out of the courtroom in one piece. On the way out of the courtroom, I ran into Aunt Bella, Jinniyah's mom. She was walking through the halls, leaving jury duty for a different case. When I saw Aunt Bella,

I just hugged her and held on tight as tears ran from my face. Uncle P's family was leaving the courtroom still celebrating his victory, while I was being consoled by Aunt Bella in my defeat.

During the trial, I felt unseen in plain sight. I was definitely in the courtroom with a judge, jury, and my free attorney explaining the hurt and pain that was inflicted on me by Uncle P, my perpetrator, by way of testifying, yet it seemed like my words fell on deaf ears. I thought I was helping other young girls by trying to get a sex offender off the streets, but I wasn't successful. It pained me to know that he was able to run free. The smiles on his face and his family's faces when he won the case hurt me deeply because I knew a truth that would leave the courtroom as a harmful lie. I felt helpless and defeated once again by Uncle P and his family. By the way, I never received my journals back after the trial. I felt betrayed, like another part of my innocence was taken without my permission. To this day, I haven't been able to write in a journal out of fear of my privacy being breached and used against me somehow throughout my life. I had been abandoned again by another family that was supposed to love and care for me. Life had a way of picking me up and letting me down, but through it all, God would never leave me alone. He continued to place people in my life that would be there to comfort and care for me when my biological family, and the foster care system would fail me. I'm grateful to know that while life is "lifing," God got me.

CHAPTER TWENTY-FOUR
SAVED BY AN ANGEL

I always believed in angels, but never saw one in person until I met this lady from church, Minister Azalea (Aunt Aza). Aunt Aza was and is the one person I could always be myself around. I didn't have to hide who I was, I didn't have to hide my past, and I didn't have to feel ashamed about my past; she allowed me and hundreds of other youth to be ourselves. Aunt Aza gave me a reason to keep pushing through life; in fact, without her, I would literally be dead, like dead, like needing to be scraped off the sidewalk dead. She was truly sent by God, exactly for me.

Late one weekend afternoon while I was away at college, during my sophomore year, I thought I had had enough of life. Life was truly getting the best of me; my emotions were all over the place. One minute I was happy, and the next I was angry, and there was no in-between. I was happy to be away at college, but angry because I felt alone in college. *I felt alone in life, period, with no one to claim me as kin.* My mental health started to fade because I didn't think I was worth anything. My mind kept telling me that no one wanted me, my mother didn't want me, my foster parents didn't want me, and the only thing I was good for was sexual pleasure. All of these feelings lead me to apply physical harm to my body. There were times I would just run into a wall to hurt myself; I'd make small cuts on my arms, take pills, or burn myself with an iron. It was like I needed to feel pain because my life was full of it, and I wasn't alive unless I felt pain. It was a tough time for me. A few weeks back, I had just gone to court to testify against the man who raped me in my foster home; having to relive that experience in front of a judge and a jury was emotionally and mentally draining. Explaining how I was raped over and over, being asked to look at Uncle P's face to point him out over and over and listening to his lawyer change my words around to fit his case and on top of that, losing the case, made me mentally unstable. I couldn't understand how the jury didn't understand the pain I lived through and the pain I was feeling at that time. I was feeling a sense of loss; not only because I lost the case, but also because every friend I had met freshman year at school, of whom all are still friends to this day, had left and gone to other colleges; even my best friend left and went to a different college.

My GPA had fallen below 2.5, and I was at risk of losing my scholarship. Although I was able to live with a friend and her family, I didn't have a family to go home to that was my own. All my other friends were getting care packages from their family members with money, and things they needed for their dorm rooms, and sometimes it made me question my reason for being. It made me question if I should be going to college at all, especially if I didn't have a place to live. I felt alone in every aspect of my life, and on this afternoon, I couldn't see how it was ever going to get better, so I decided I was going to kill myself. With tears in my eyes, I pondered *If I killed myself, I wouldn't have to worry about anything or anyone. No one would miss me; I'm just a burden on everyone I encounter; the world would be better without me in it.* In cartoons and movies, when a person is having an internal conflict, it gives the depiction of a devil on the left shoulder and an angel on the right shoulder, and the person is going back and forth between bad and good thoughts. My case was different; there was a devil on my left and right shoulder encouraging me to kill myself, reminding me of how hopeless and useless I was to the world. Nothing good could come out of my thoughts at this time; I was done fighting for my life and wanted it to be over.

The fourth floor of my dorm building was almost empty due to students going home on the weekends. I preferred not to go home on weekends, so I didn't feel like a burden on the family — Jinniyah's family. Even though I loved and still love to this day her family, it was hard for me to accept the love they gave me because I didn't think I deserved their love. *How could a girl like me, with no biological family, a girl who has been pushed around physically and sexually, deserve a family to love me?* were my thoughts when I went home on break. I started to think of ways I could kill myself and be successful. The last time I tried to kill myself by taking pills, it didn't work; I just wound up with a huge migraine. This time, I had to do something that was sure to do the job. *I could use a pair of scissors and try to slit my wrists again,* I thought, but I was too chicken to do it. I would feel the pain, and I wouldn't be able to go through with it as soon as the scissors pressed up against my skin. I walked out into the hallway of my dorm and paced the halls for a little. The hallway was about 200 feet long by 10 feet wide with about 15 rooms on either side of the walls. There were restrooms in the middle of the hall on the left side of the dorm hallway, which was directly across from the middle staircase on the right side of the hall facing the restrooms. Going down through the double doors to get to the staircase was a landing followed by about 10 stairs and another landing with a window about 5 ft long and 5 ft wide in front of the landing. I decided to walk down the stairs to the landing, where the window was, and just peer out of the window. At first, I went there to think about how I was going to kill myself, and then a thought came to my mind to jump. I heard the voice in my head, clear as day, saying, *"You should jump."* I stepped back from the window, spooked out, but also interested in the plan. *Jump, you will definitely die if you jump off the fourth floor of a dormitory building,* I heard. I walked myself back to the window, looking out of it, to analyze the fall and calculate the ways it would or would not work. *It looks high; I could die, or I would hurt myself badly,* and the thoughts ran through my mind. I knew that if I didn't die, I would have failed another suicide attempt, but this time I could potentially end up deformed for the rest of my life, *which would defeat the purpose.* I thought of ways I could jump out of the window to make it so that I couldn't break my fall. *I could just sit in the window with my legs hanging, lean forward, and belly flop straight on my face, that would surely flatline me.* I thought as I looked out of the window and down to the concrete ground. I just needed to get over the initial fear of pulling this off because I was afraid of heights.

My mind was made up; I was going to sit in the window with both legs hanging out, close my eyes, count to 3, and lean forward out of the window. The only thing that was left to do was leave a note behind for anyone who wanted to read it. *Should I leave a note behind? No one cares,* I thought. To me, leaving a note meant someone cared for you. It meant you had people who loved you, people that would want to know why you killed yourself, and at the time, I didn't feel like I had anyone that would care or understand, so I quickly ditched the thought of writing a note. As I started to climb through the window, my cell phone rang. I had that good ole Nokia phone that was loud and sturdy. The Nokia ringtone sang *di ti ni ni, di ti ni ni, di ti ni ni niiiii* through the air as the phone vibrated in my pocket, where it was neglected the whole time, I plotted my fate. I reached into my pocket to get my cell phone, looked at the caller ID, and it was Aunt Aza. Aunt Aza rarely called me while I was at college, so I had to pick it up. Although I was ready to end my life, I couldn't ignore Aunt Aza's call; it just wouldn't be right, so I picked up the phone, and her sweet voice saved my life.

"Hey baby, what you doing?" Aunt Aza asked.

"Hi, Aunt Aza, I am OK" I lied, fighting back tears, so that she wouldn't figure me out.

"You don't sound alright. What are you doing?" she asked again, as if she knew what I was doing. I looked around, up in the air, and out of the window, knowing I was alone, but wondering what she knew. *How did she know what I was thinking, or doing?*

I hesitantly responded, "I am looking out of the window," which technically wasn't a lie because her phone call had stopped me from sitting in the window.

"Were you thinking about jumping?" Aunt Aza said in her angelic voice. I couldn't lie too much to her because it felt like a sin. I mean, it is a sin to lie to anyone, and I was okay with lying to anyone else, but not to Aunt Aza; that was a sin, a big sin.

"Yes, I don't want to be here anymore; it's too hard!" I said this in a breakdown of uncontrollable tears.

"Listen to me, baby; I know you are going through a lot right now, but God still loves you and I love you, so I need you to go to your room, and I will be there to pick you up," Aunt Aza said in a calm tone, after clearing the knot in her throat.

I whimpered, "I don't know if I could handle all this, Aunt Aza; you saw what happened in the courtroom. I don't belong here; everywhere I go, I mess up, and everyone winds up hating me!"

"Baby, some people hate themselves and then take their hate out on other people. Tameena, you didn't do anything wrong, and surely didn't deserve to be treated the way you were treated. I am on my way; come down to the front with a bag. You can stay for the weekend with me, okay. I love you!" Aunt Aza reassured me.

"Ok, I love you too!" I replied as I backed away from the window and walked up the last flight of stairs to go to my room.

"Stay on the phone with me baby; I am almost there," she instructed.

I put my phone down while I packed a small bag of clothes. Only a few minutes went by before I started crying again and talking to myself, *this is too much; wait how did she know I was? ... why do I feel so much pain?* I couldn't complete a thought! *I even forgot I was on the phone with my aunt,* I thought aloud.

"No worries baby. I am here!" she said.

"You're here already? It's only been 20 minutes since you called!" I said, confused about how she arrived so quickly. Aunt Aza lived in Philly an hour away from Lincoln University. I still don't know how she got there so quickly.

"Yeah, baby, I was already on the road when I called you; something told me to come and get you this weekend. I was going to surprise you, but then I decided to call so you would be ready!" And just like that, I was saved by an earthly angel. Aunt Aza arrived at the front door of my dorm building, and I hopped in her car, feeling like I was leaving everything behind. On the ride, we talked about how and what I was feeling. I was so overwhelmed with different emotions that my mind shut off within 10 minutes of the ride, and then I fell asleep until I reached Aunt Aza's apartment.

Aunt Aza let me sleep until we reached her house, and then she fed me, and prayed for me; talked to me, and afterward, I got more rest.

Looking back on that night, I realized that I was loved and that someone did care about me, even if it was just Aunt Aza. Her love was enough to make anyone feel safe and wanted. She could make you feel loved and wanted by God and loved and wanted by her presence. More importantly, I felt loved by God. God was so gracious towards me that he sent his earthly angel to come to see about me and save me from myself. I'm reminded of a song by Helen Baylor that sings, "If it had not been, for the Lord on my side, tell me where would I be? Where would I be?" I know for a fact that I would be dead if it wasn't for him strategically placing Aunt Aza in my life. Not only was Aunt Aza there for me in my lowest need, but she also took me under her wing after that episode. She continued to call and check on me. She let me stay at her house; I babysat her children. She answered my calls no matter the time of day or night. Meeting Aunt Aza was one of the most amazing things that ever happened in my life.

IT HAD TO HAPPEN

CHAPTER TWENTY-FIVE
SUMMERS WITH THE MOORE FAMILY

It was the last few weeks of summer before I left for college when I moved in with Tattiana. Like every move I've ever had, I moved into Tattiana's house with my trash bags as suitcases. My Aunt Sandi picked me up from Ms. Joanne's house and dropped me off at Tattiana's. I was greeted by her mother (Aunt Jenny), who told me, "Come on in and get comfortable; you're part of the family now," and she gave me a hug. I was so happy but nervous at the same time because, in the back of my head, I heard, *come on in, but don't get too comfortable because we know how this ends.* In certain situations, my head raced with its own train of thoughts most of the time, and most days, my thoughts put me in a fight or flight mode. On this day, I chose to fight, not physically, but for my need, which was shelter.

So, during the greeting, I nodded and smiled and responded, "Thank you so much, Aunt Jenny. When I get a job, I can pay you something for letting me live with you," while returning a big hug.

"Girl, I said you're family now. You don't have to pay to live here," Aunt Jenny said.

"Thank you again," I responded, feeling homeless and humble.

Tattiana lived with her mother (Aunt Jenny), father (Uncle Lou), younger sister (Marcy), younger brother (LJ), and her godmom (Aunt Magy). They lived in a 3-bedroom house with a livable basement. Aunt Jenny and Uncle Lou slept in the master bedroom towards the front of the house, and Tatittiana slept in the middle room by herself. Marcy and LJ slept in a room with a set of bunk beds, and the basement was where Aunt Magy lived. The first week, I slept on the couch because they didn't have an extra bedroom for me. Sleeping on the couch brought me nightmares of the last time I slept on someone's couch; the man of the house would stare at me while I slept. There were times I'd wake up and see him standing right over me, looking down at me. He never touched me or anything, but he would just be watching me; *some people are just creepy*. Without sharing this information with Tattiana, I asked her if I could sleep in the room with her, and she said yes. Her room was small; we shared her twin-size bed for about a week and realized that wasn't going to work. Ms. Jenny had a mattress that no one was using and put it on the floor next to Tattiana's bed, and I started to sleep on the mattress on the floor. It wasn't ideal, but it was my own bed and space, and I was content. Besides, Tattiana and I had lots of fun conversations during bedtime. It would be dark in the room, and we would just talk about everything and everybody until we fell asleep. I was happy I had a place to lay my head.

If you know me, you know my cleaning is different. I worked like Cinderella at my mother's house, and honey, I cleaned, cleaned. I started cleaning, like I used to do when I was younger. Maybe I was just looking for something to do to pay Tattiana's family back. Since I knew Aunt Jenny wouldn't charge me to live there, I decided I was going to clean my way through as my contribution to living rent-free. Moving in with Tattiana made me so nervous and anxious. I thought somehow, I would mess things up with her and her family and be put out in the streets, and worst of all, our friendship would end. After all, I wasn't just good at cleaning, it seemed like I was good at pissing people off and causing them to disown me. I didn't want it to happen this time. This time I had to make sure I was perfect and humble to be part of the family without making any mistakes. I had to make sure I didn't dress too revealingly because I didn't want Tattiana's father or brother to look at me in inappropriate ways. Even though they never looked at me in that way, I was guarded; my past experiences wouldn't let me believe that it would never happen again. It was my way of protecting myself and Tattiana's family as well. My mindset was to be pleasant and always get along with everyone, never showing discomfort or disappointment with anyone. I thought I had to just go with the flow.

I was in survival mode, but it wasn't long before I started to feel like I was part of the Moore Family, even if it was only in the summers during school break.

Tatiana and Jinniyah went everywhere together. When I saw them in church, they were always together, but seeing them outside of church, I realized they started their days together and ended their days together. They were like sister cousins because where you saw Tattiana, you saw Jinniyah. In the morning, they would call each other, and we'd all make plans for what we were going to do that day, and we'd meet up to get our day started. Tattiana and Jinniyah took me to their grandma's block in West Philly where most of their friends lived. Jinniyah introduced me to their friends as one of their cousins; "This is my cousin, Meena," she would say when she introduced me to her crew. Now, I just went with the flow, but in my mind, it felt good to be claimed as part of their family. I was longing to be part of a family so badly, that they could have introduced me as their pet, and I would've been satisfied. Everyone in their crew was cool; they accepted me as if I grew up with them, like Tattiana and Jinniyah. We would hang out in West Philly all day, walking the streets, going to different friends' houses, and eating at Mimmo's, or going to the Papi stores. Mimmo's cheese fries were so good; I think we went there almost every day. In West Philly, it was always something to do and someplace to be when I hung out with Tattiana and Jinniyah. Hanging with them showed me how close-knit their entire family was with each other.

The Moore family was unlike any other family I had ever met. They seemed happy to be around each other, and they seemed functional. Every Sunday after church, they would have Sunday dinner with almost the entire family at Grandma's (Jinniyah and Tattiana's grandma) house. Grandma had six children, represented by five households, including husbands, wives, grandchildren, and me. There would be at least thirty people at Sunday dinner every Sunday. At first, it was a little overwhelming for me to be around the whole family like that because I felt out of place, and it made me think about my own family. Sunday dinners in some ways made me depressed; it made me not want to be around the whole family, but I pushed through, and the more I went, the more I grew to love the Moore family. Besides, Grandma would cook a nice spread of mac & cheese, collard greens, yams, chicken, ribs or fish, rice, and whatever other soul food ingredient you could think of, and it was good. She made different desserts, like sweet potato pie, a variety of cakes, and cookies, and we would have some type of ice cream. There was no way I was going to pass up all that good food, and in some ways, it reminded me of my mother's cooking. Now, my mother could cook, but Grandma threw it down, and she did it every Sunday. My mother only cooked on special occasions. For

Grandma, it didn't need to be a holiday like Thanksgiving or some special occasion for the family to get together. Sundays were a special occasion for family time where everyone could get together to talk, laugh, and eat. Not only did the family meet every Sunday, but they took a week of family vacation during the summer every summer.

The summer after my sophomore year of college, I went on my first family vacation with the Moore Family, and it was super fun and free! I did not pay a penny; all expenses were paid for me by Aunt Jenny. It was so amazing to me that I would be included in the family vacation plans for free. The Moore family knew how to make me feel like I belonged as part of their family. We went to Myrtle Beach, South Carolina, for about seven days. The entire family stayed in the same hotel, but each individual family group stayed in the same room. I stayed in a room with Tattiana's family because that's who I was living with at the time. Most of the time, we did whole family activities like Beach Day, and we went to a few museums as a family, but on some days, the children all hung out together. Tattiana, Jinniyah, and I stayed together each day of the trip, walking the strip and meeting people. On the second night of Myrtle Beach, we met these boys who were from Atlanta and were trying to holla (talk to us in a getting-to-know-us way) at us so we could hang out with them. The boys were from our hotel, and we did meet up a few times just to entertain them a little. We were all talking by the pool when they started singing songs that Tattiana, Jinniyah, and I had never heard before, like my favorite song, "Laffy Taffy" by D4L. They sang with their thick, down-south accents, ("Girl shake dat laffy taffy, dat laffy taffy, shake dat laffy taffy, dat laffy taffy, girl,"). The rest of the song was about female features and body parts represented by different types of candy. It was wild to hear those boys with their country accents singing such a crazy but catchy song. The girls and I were laughing, singing, and dancing along with them, having a good time with these strangers for the remainder of our vacation.

On one of the days we were there, all of the children (cousins) went in the outdoor hotel pool to play beach ball. I wore a dookie green two-piece bathing suit. *I don't know why I called it dookie green, but maybe a dark olive green.* The top was securely

336

tied at the back of my neck and to the middle part of my back. *At least, I thought it was securely tied* until I jumped for the beach ball and my top had lifted above my breast, exposing my itty-bitty boobs. What made it worse was that I didn't even realize my top lifted as I continued to jump up and down in the water, flashing everyone with my boobs. Jinniyah and Tattitana were trying to get my attention by pointing at me, signaling for me to fix my top. When I looked down, I saw both boobs out, and I was so embarrassed. Everyone was laughing, so I laughed it off too, but I was embarrassed because there were like three or four boy cousins in the pool with us that saw my little boobs. I kind of beat myself up about it for the rest of the trip because I kept thinking about what the cousins thought of me. *I hope they don't think I did it on purpose; I hope my boy cousins don't tease me about this and make it more uncomfortable, I hope they don't try to touch me inappropriately after this.* By this time, it had been a mental struggle for me. In my head, I was going through a lot and hoped I didn't start the beginning of the end of my relationship with the Moore Family because I accidentally flashed my boobs. Although none of the above thoughts came to pass, my first family vacation with the Moore family was fun with a splash of embarrassment and shame. The next summer vacation was even more fun and a lot less embarrassing.

When I came home from Lincoln after my junior year of college, it was vacation time again. I went to Canada with the Moore's. The process was fun because I got my first passport for the vacation. Originally, we were supposed to go to Jamaica, but those plans changed because everyone's passports did not arrive in time. Instead of wasting the week, we chose to go to Canada. I was then years old when I found out that Canada was its own country, even though it was connected to the United States of America. I learned that we could use our passports to cross the border, and if we didn't have them, we could use the receipt for purchasing our passport along with our state IDs. My passport came in time, and it felt so good to see Canada stamped on my passport because it indicated that I had been out of the country, and that was an amazing feeling. Never in a thousand years did I ever think I was going to be able to visit another country. As a former foster child, the statistics didn't talk much about the possibility of foster children finding a family that would care for them and take them on vacations. I just didn't know if it could happen for me or to me. Foster children usually get sent to respite care when the foster family goes on vacation. Thankfully, I got to go on vacation because Canada was a blast. It was about an 8-hour drive filled with sleep, laughter, food and snacks, and rest stops. Niagara Falls, Canada was beautiful, and the people were so kind with their Canadian accents — ay — and their smiling faces. We visited Niagara Falls, and we did a lot of sightseeing. On one trip, we boarded the Maid of the Mist (the boat) to get as close to the Falls as we could. It was beautiful and a little chilly. We wore blue rain ponchos to keep us from getting wet from the mist of the Falls. While I was in the boat, I looked at all the beautiful blue water around me and the beautiful waterfalls, and I could not help but thank God for this wonderful opportunity to travel with the Moore family and to experience such a beautiful sight as well as other experiences. Something in me wanted to let my guard down, to make me aware of my safety, and to give me a sense of belonging to this family, but deep down inside I couldn't. *Nothing was ever this good for long,* I thought, but I embraced the beautiful moment I was in and decided to just go with the flow. Niagara Falls was beautiful, but it wasn't the highlight of the vacation; the family rap was hands down the best part.

We were eating at a restaurant in Canada, and I can't remember the exact restaurant, but as usual, the Moore Family was squad deep. There were at least twenty of us in this restaurant eating, laughing, and having a great time. Our waitress wasn't the best; I don't think she knew how to serve such a large crowd, and she kept getting our orders wrong or coming out too late with our orders. I don't remember who noticed, but the waitress's shoes were untied the entire time she waited on us. The Moore Family are great tippers; *if you are a waiter or waitress, you want to make sure you serve our table because we gonna tip you good.* If it's one thing about the Moore's, they love great customer service and are willing to tip well in response. When we finished eating and the adults started to talk about the level of service and what they should tip the waitress, Jinniyah blurted out, "I got a tip for her; she needs to tie her shoes! That's why she was so slow, because her shoes are untied!" and everyone started cracking up laughing. The waitress wasn't around when Jinniyah said it, but when she came back to our table and was standing around like she was waiting for a tip, Jinniyah rhythmically said, "Tie your shoe," and the whole table started cracking up again. It was so funny, and somehow that statement became the hook for the rap by the Moore's. The rap had about ten to twelve verses because we were all just making up rhymes to a beat, and everyone's verse had to end with the hook "tie your shoe, tie your shoe, tie your shoe, tie your shoe." I can't remember everyone's rap verse, but I remember a little bit about mine, *which may be a little bit of someone's part, too, but it's not like they could sue me lol,* but it went, "Chillin' in Canada, my bathing suit popping. Walking down the street, all the boys keep stopping. The boys said, 'Girl, you fine cause you got me tripping.' I said, 'Nah, you tripping cause your shoelaces slipping,' tie your shoe, tie your shoe, tie your shoe, tie your shoe" and the family went wild, cheering, laughing. Tattiana's verse was, "Walking down the street as fly as can be, then I see a dude tryna holla at me. I walked over there to see what he was spitting, I looked down and saw that his shoelaces slipping, tie your shoe, tie your shoe, tie your shoe, tie your shoe." It was a very good

341

time, and just so you know, we did tip the waitress well. Canada was a perfect vacation because I didn't flash anyone with my boobs. When it came to vacations, the Bahamas was even better; *I still can't believe they took me to the Bahamas.*

My senior year of college was ending, and like every other summer vacation, I didn't know anything about what was going on until I got home from Lincoln. This summer vacation was held in the Bahamas, and my portion was paid! I could not believe that the family paid for my trip because there was a lot involved. We weren't just driving somewhere; we caught a plane and got on a boat to get to the Bahamas. That was so much money; I felt bad for not being able to pay my own way. I felt like I was a burden on the family, but in the back of my mind somewhere, I knew that if they didn't want me there, they would not have paid my way to go. My pride and ego were hurt, but my spirit was once again happy to be part of the family and actually doing things the family did without being sent to respite care. I had to change my thinking and tell myself that *what the Moore family was doing for me was out of the kindness of their hearts, and not to make me feel bad.* After the plane ride, we got on

342

a ferry that took us to the Bahamas. The ferry had games, activities, food, and drinks that kept us occupied with fun-filled things to do until we made it to our final destination, Freeport, Bahamas!

Freeport, Bahamas was beautiful, and the beachside resort we stayed in was just fabulous. When we got to the resort, we were greeted with cool towels and drinks while we waited for our rooms to become available. As a family, we went on excursions and met up for dinner each night. As always, Jinniyah, Tattitana, and a few other cousins and I would venture off to see what we could get into, looking for some fun teenage things to participate in. The adults gave us a late curfew (1 a.m.!) as long as we stayed at the resort. That was enough time for us to find a club and get our party on. The vacation highlight for the teens was the club. It was Tattiana, Jinniyah, their cousin Rodney, and I who found this small bar. I believed I was the only legal person to get into this club, but the owner of the bar let us all in. The music was awesome; the beats, the songs, and the dancing were all so cool. We learned different dances from the bar owner, who seemed to be into me. He kept giving me alcoholic drinks for free, as well as Tattiana, Jinniyah, and Rodney.

343

I don't know if he was trying to get us drunk for some bad reason or if he just wanted us to have a good time, but at the moment, we kept drinking and dancing. Tattiana and Jinniyah met some guys in the club as well; they were eyeing them and kept trying to dance with them all night. Most of the night, we danced with the guys, and Rodney danced with a few girls. By the end of the night, we were all so drunk, but we stayed together to make sure nothing happened to any of us. Of all the other vacations I went on with the Moore family, the Bahamas was the most fun. Some of my best and favorite memories during this period of my life were the times I spent with the Moore family. I couldn't have asked for a different family to make me happy the way this family made me happy. I am forever grateful to God for leading me to them and grateful to the family for choosing me to be part of such an amazing and loving family. I love you all!

CHAPTER TWENTY-SIX
SENIOR YEAR

Senior year was so much fun, but very emotional at the same time. I always loved going back to campus because, although I knew Neka's family didn't mind me staying with them during the summer months, I felt like they deserved the next nine months off from taking care of an extra child. Besides, being away at school gave me a sense of independence that I needed to make me feel better about my life's abandonment issues. It was like a trial run of how things would be on my own when I graduated, *minus the free room and board*. Also, it felt good going back to campus to meet up with my friends, which felt like a little family in itself because we have known each other for the past four years. I had accumulated a few different groups of friends based on all the groups, sports, and other activities I participated in, so I was kind of popular because I knew a lot of people. I played volleyball all four years, managed the women's basketball team all four years, sang on the Lincoln University Gospel Choir (LUGC) all four years, danced on the Lincoln University Dance Ministry (LUDM) all four years, and

345

became an adjutant in training for the Chaplain at the college. Each group of friends had a different impact on my time at Lincoln, which I loved dearly. I tried to keep myself busy so I wouldn't focus on the wantonness I was dealing with throughout the school years and the anticipated despair that was to come after I graduated.

The excitement of being a senior on campus gave me a boost of confidence that I was destined for greatness, but knowing that in the next few months, I would be graduating and separating from yet another family for good was a little saddening. I started the year out strong, wanting to do my best so that I could feel good about how I finished my senior year. Why *do we do this? We play around too much all the other years, and then suddenly, in our senior year, we come to our senses as if our other years don't count towards our overall GPA.* Anyway, when it came to socializing, I was the one who did the most during my college years, jeopardizing my scholarship and degree, but I got it together. Realizing that for me, the stakes were a lot higher than for my friends. They were going back home to *their* families, security, and unconditional love; I was going back to *someone else's* home to live with *someone else's* family. To me, and based on my past experiences in other homes,

The Moore's involvement was conditional; the duration of their care

for me depended on my behavior, and my ability to keep quiet if

anything went wrong. So, I went into senior year with goals that I

would graduate and pass each class with A's and Bs to help bring

up that 2.5 to at least a 3.0 GPA. In my mind, if I got a 3.0, I would

be able to get a good job to care for myself after graduation. If you

went to college, you know that a GPA is like the Life Alert

commercial, "I've fallen and I can't get up." Once that GPA goes

down, it's very hard to get it back up. I had to make a plan to get

my GPA up; *I needed that Life Alert Pendant.* Of course, college

was bombarding seniors with parties and social gatherings, but I

missed out on some so I could focus on my goal. I went to study

halls that were offered all four years, but I just decided senior year

would be a great time to utilize the resource. It wasn't long before

reality started kicking in and affecting me emotionally and mentally,

and before long, I stopped going to study hall and hanging out with

my friends.

Disappointments started to roll in during my senior year; they were coming in from the left and right. My good friend, Sasha, and I were the team captains on the volleyball team, and we were invited to join a national volleyball team abroad. Around the end of the season, our coach handed Sasha and me the invitation, and we were both so excited to be eligible to play abroad. It was going to be a traveling team where we would travel to Spain, the Netherlands, and a few other countries. In that moment, I felt a sense of worthiness that I could do something great for myself. In that moment, it felt like such an honor to be looked at and given the opportunity, so much that I forgot my current situation. My coach, the team, Sasha, and I celebrated at the invitation, but it wasn't until I saw the amount of money I would have to pay to join the travel team that I knew I was not going to be able to go. The cost was $2,000 to attend, and I knew for a fact that I wasn't going to be able to go because I couldn't afford to pay $2,000, at least not from my work-study job. Sasha was able to ask her parents, but they refused. There was no one for me to ask at the time. I wasn't a ward of the state anymore, and I wasn't officially moved in with Neeka's family; college was my home. When Sasha told me the news that her parents wouldn't pay for her to go, I lied and told her my parents said the same thing. I silently thought, *at least she had someone to ask.* That moment started the downward spiral of disappointment for me.

I became depressed about not being able to play volleyball abroad**,** so at that point, I started to smoke and drink alcohol on campus again. There were a few friends whom I knew from class that smoked weed, so during my depressed times, I would link up and hang with them. I knew I could get high and drunk with them, and on them (meaning I didn't have to pay). *I couldn't afford any weed or alcohol, and even if I could, I didn't have a car to get it, but my friends did — don't judge me; love me y'all.* Meanwhile, my schoolwork was still important to me, so I was still completing my work and still working towards my goal. During the day, I would do my work and then after I finished, I would go to parties with my friends. I would get high, get drunk, chill at night, and then repeat. Smoking and drinking were a temporary fix to help me to stop thinking about my misfortune future. I started having mental breakdowns in my dorm room when I would feel alone and unwanted. Everything made me feel bad about myself; these sensitivities, like listening to a friend talk on the phone with their parents, watching students pick up packages from their mailboxes, and seeing family members visit their child's games during the year, later caused mental breakdowns. Jinniyah and Tattiana started visiting me to watch a few of my volleyball games, but I suspected it was just them wanting to go to a college campus and have fun with college kids. They were still in high school, so they loved it when they came to get a feel for what living on campus was like. Outwardly, I had so much fun when they came, but deep inside, I didn't feel like they came in the spirit of support for me, and they were young, so it wasn't necessarily their job to make me feel supported. I worked through my issues by crying, trashing my room, and breaking my things when I had alone time. I would have a moment, then I would be fine again, ready to reach my senior year goal.

Despite all of the lows I experienced in my senior year, the one high I was looking forward to was reaching my goal of graduating with a 3.0 or higher. I finished and passed all my classes with A's and Bs as planned, but my GPA only rose to 2.83. *I told y'all about those GPAs, I should've yelled, "HELP, I'VE FALLEN AND I CAN'T GET UP."* This made me feel insecure about myself because I really wanted to get a 3.0; *I thought I would never be able to get a good job, and that would have been on me.* Everything people said about me, about how I wasn't going to be anything, was setting in. My mind started replaying disappointing moments of me getting expelled from elementary and middle school, the moment I had to beg my scholarship representative to let me keep my scholarship. I was in jeopardy of losing it because I wasn't doing my best. It was hard to handle that I was the one screwing up my life this time, not my mother nor the foster care system; it was me. When I saw my transcript, I had a breakdown in my dorm room because it was bad. I punched the walls, kicked, and broke my closet door, and I sobbed until I came to my senses. After I finished punching and breaking my things, a thought came to me, *Meena, at least you are graduating!* I was going to be the first in my family to graduate college; It didn't matter what GPA I graduated with, I was excited to graduate. I started to feel a little good about myself again. I literally had a bipolar moment where I got up off the floor, started cleaning up, and laughed at myself for making such a mess. My knuckles hurt and my closet door was broken, but I was getting ready for senior week.

Senior week is the last week on campus, which is only for graduating seniors. It was a week full of seniors getting ready for graduation by going to get our caps and gowns, attending graduation practice, getting our final transcripts, handling any financial debts owed at the bursar's office, and partying each night. It was so exciting and emotional because this was the last week I'd get to hang out with my friends before starting our adult lives. The first day of the senior week was an information day about what to expect during the week, and then there was a party. After the information session, I hung out with my friends, and we went to the party. I had a ball; I had a little to drink but danced a lot. Day two of senior week was when the seniors had to meet with the Bursar's office to make sure that final tuition was paid because if you owed tuition, you would not be able to graduate. The good thing for me is that my tuition was paid on time every year by my scholarship representative. Caps and gowns were given out on day two, and it made me feel accomplished. This was going to be my first major accomplishment and one step forward to making a better life for myself. I started to see the light at the end of the long and dreadful tunnel I had been climbing my way out of all my life. My friends and I were taking turns having sleepovers in each other's dorms; we spent as much time together as we could. We had so much fun, and I couldn't wait to see what day three was going to bring. On day three, my bright future started to dim. I found out that the light I thought I saw was not at the end of the tunnel — it was just a hole, for ahead of me was a lot more tunnel to go.

Day three of senior week consisted of getting graduation announcements (tickets) for family and friends to attend the graduation, which made me feel sad. I had a family to give my announcements to, but it just wouldn't be my family. Nevertheless, I was excited to be able to invite Jinniyah and Tattiana's family to my graduation; at least, I knew they were going to come. I went to the student union building (The SUB) with my friends to pick up our announcements together. I was with my six church friends, and I was the fourth in line to make it to the front. My three friends went, and they were in and out. When I got up to the front of the line, the lady asked, "Name please." I responded, "Tameena Hill," excited to get my tickets. The lady looked over all the envelopes with students' names on them, all in alphabetical order by last name. *I noticed because I was watching her look for my name.* My name didn't show up, even as she looked for a second time.

"I don't see your name here. Have you spoken to your academic advisor yet to make sure you are graduating?" she said, looking me straight in the eyes.

"No, I haven't yet, but I received the email saying, 'Congratulations, Senior on your upcoming graduation!' with the packet of information about graduation," I said assuredly.

"I understand, but I do not have announcements for you here. You may want to check with your academic advisor and then come back when everything is settled. NEXT!" she said, signaling for one of my friends who was behind me.

I was so frustrated because everything was going well, and then all of a sudden, an issue arose to knock me off my block. I told my friends I would meet up with them later after I spoke with my academic advisor and got everything cleared up and situated.

Immediately after leaving the SUB, I went to my academic advisor in the education department. I walked into her room and said, "Hi Ms. Glout, I went to the SUB to get my announcements for graduation, but they didn't have an envelope for me, and they told me to come see you." Ms. Glout was also my special education teacher for some of my classes. She had dyslexia, which she announced to the class very often to prove that students with special needs can grow to be successful as she did. One semester, Ms. Clout gave me a D as the final grade, and I didn't understand why. When I approached her about my grade, it was because she had gotten me mixed up with another student. I was supposed to have a B. It took Ms. Glout weeks before she fixed my grade in the system. I was hoping she didn't mix me up again with anyone else, because I needed to graduate, or better yet, she did mix me up with someone else, and it could be fixed so I could graduate.

"Tameena, it says here that you are missing one credit," my advisor said, turning her computer around for me to see.

"What do you mean I'm missing one credit? I've taken every course that was required in my major." I responded with worry in my throat.

"You're not necessarily missing a required class, but a required credit, your elective. You didn't take an elective, which is only worth one credit. You need to take a one-credit course in the summer," my advisor explained.

"In the summer! You mean to tell me that after I graduate, I have to come back for one credit, even though I have extra credits in other subjects? Can I use the extra credits that I have toward an elective? That way, I don't have to come back after graduation." I asked with hope in my voice.

It was the university's policy for the past few years that students would be able to graduate with their class if they were missing a class or 3 credits, but they would have to do summer school to make up that class and would not receive their diploma until they passed the class in the summer. I was annoyed because I didn't plan on going to summer school. I wanted to be done with college but didn't get too upset because I knew the university would let me walk across the stage on graduation day without receiving my actual degree until I finished the course in the summer, but of course, the policy changed that year.

"Ms. Glout, but I would be able to graduate even if I'm missing a credit, so why didn't they have my announcements?" I asked.

"Tameena, the policy has changed; Lincoln University does not allow students to graduate if they are missing anything." Ms. Glout answered, sounding sorry for me.

"So why didn't you tell me about this credit before now? You're my academic advisor; you should have known this so I could have made it up," I blamed.

She kindly responded, "Tameena, you are right; I should have seen it, but you should have checked as well. I'm sorry, dear; you must complete the summer class and then graduate next May," she said, dismissing me from her office.

"This some bullshit," I snapped as I left her office.

I was so disappointed in myself and embarrassed to tell anyone what was going on, so I went to my room and snapped out. I started screaming and yelling, "This some bullshit," knocking over everything I owned, picking up things, and breaking and throwing them around the room. *What am I going to do now? How am I going to take care of myself if I can't get a degree?* I thought to myself. My mind was racing a mile a minute, trying to figure out why these kinds of things happen to me. What will I tell Jinniyah and Tattiana's family? What will I tell my friends? *Why am I here if nothing will go right for me?* I thought to myself and suicide glanced across my mind. I felt like a huge failure and started to accept the stereotypes that were placed on children that were in foster care. *Did you know that, according to the U.S. Department of Education, 400,00 children and youth are in foster care at any given time over the course of their lives? Only 3% of those children move on to graduate from college. It is expected that children who were in foster care will grow up to be in jail or homeless by their adult years.* The odds were always stacked against me, so the thought of suicide crossed my mind for a hot second, I thought about taking myself out of there, but I promised Aunt Aza I would never try to kill myself again. Instead, I decided I was going to keep this between me, myself, and I for now and tell my friends later. My mind told me to get high and drink before going to the party that night, and that's exactly what I did, before meeting up with my friends.

My friends came by to pick me up from my dorm room, and I was *nice* (just feeling the alcohol kick in, but not drunk). We all walked to the dorm where the party was going on, and basically it was like one floor where the seniors lived. Everyone had their dorm rooms open for anyone to come in and access whatever — drinks, weed, dancing, etc. The only lights that were on were the hallway lights of the dorm floor. In every room, there were party lights, stereo lights, and disco looking lights. I could tell the students had put a lot of thought into this because I felt like I was at a club when I went into each room. Everyone was singing and dancing, and there were fraternities and sororities line dancing while drinks were being made and blunts were being burned and passed. My friends and I were having so much fun, going to each room, drinking, and having a good time. We stayed together for most of the night to make sure everyone was accounted for before we went back to our dorm rooms for the night, except that I somehow ventured off to a room with a friend from class. He was Hispanic, light-skinned, with nice hair; he was a little thick, and he dressed nice. I walked into his room, which had a lot of people in it, when he grabbed me and we started dancing. He gave me a few drinks while we were dancing, and I think he could tell I was already drunk because he started kissing me and touching me, and *it was feeling good.* I ain't even gonna lie; he almost got me with his cute self, but my friends came in the room looking for me. My friend Deannah grabbed my hand, and we left the room. At this point, I stumbled out of that room and into my friend's hands. My friends noticed that I was really drunk, and they had to take me back to my dorm because I was tripping. After that, I don't remember what happened for the rest of the night; I just know I was with my friends and in good hands. I went to sleep and woke up on Day four.

Day four, I woke up with all my friends in my room and a huge headache. They were telling me stories of how I was dancing and picking fights with people until they decided it was time for me to go to my room. I just came out and told them, "I'm not graduating this year," I whispered. "They said I'm missing a credit and that I wouldn't be able to graduate; I would have to take a class over the summer and graduate next year," I continued.

"That's crazy; I'm so sorry," Deannah said.

"Well, we gonna party today for you, Meena," my friend Tyler said.

"It's okay, I'm gonna call my aunt to come get me today," I whispered with tears in my eyes.

All my friends surrounded me, hugging and kissing me. They were so sad for me; just as sad as I was for myself. I called Tattiana's mom to explain to her my situation and that I needed to get picked up to go home. I had two more days left of Senior Week, but I was so depressed I couldn't stay; I had to get picked up. Tattiana's mom said that she couldn't come and get me that day, that I had to wait until the next day, and she would be there to pick me up. So, I stayed and partied with my friends all that night, enjoying my last night with my friends, and the next day got picked up. The whole family came — Tattiana's mom, Aunt Jennifer (Aunt Jenny), Jinniyah's mom, Aunt Bella, and the rest of the family. They all rolled up in a few cars to come support me even though they knew I wasn't graduating. This is when I really felt accepted and loved by my newly adopted, *not adopted,* family because they showed up for me during one of the most hurtful and disappointing times in my life. I left campus not achieving any of my goals for senior year. However, I took a road trip with the family to Baltimore, Maryland, eagerly anticipating another amazing summer with the Moore's.

www.ingramcontent.com/pod-product-compliance
Lightning Source LLC
Chambersburg PA
CBHW071135130626
46553CB00004B/1389